Racing Dinghy Sails

By the same author:

Teach Your Child About Sailing (*C. Arthur Pearson Ltd*)
Sails (*Adlard Coles Ltd*)
Out in Front (sailing film by *ICI Fibres Ltd*) Technical Adviser

Contents

Introduction

When I was originally asked by Adlard Coles Ltd in 1966 to write a book about sails, I was told to produce 'the best and most complete work on the subject in the English language'; the result was *Sails*, published some time ago at 65s. Whether it is the best is not for me to judge; I do claim, however, that it is the most complete. Unfortunately this means that it does cost rather a lot.

There is a demand for a cheaper work, restricted to racing dinghies, with no frills or long-winded technicalities. This book tries to answer that need and, although it naturally covers some of the same ground as *Sails*, it uses a lot of drawings to make things clear, it is a good deal crisper, and it 'tells it like it is'.

I'm sorry for any omissions; the nature of the book keeps out any attempt at elaboration or side issues. If you want more of anything, you'll have to buy *Sails*, which has something to say about nearly every aspect of the subject regarding dinghies as well as bigger boats; I think you will find it worth its price.

Sails are the power unit of a sailing boat, which wouldn't get far without them. It pays to know about them.

1 Theory

No serious examination of sails, their behaviour, and the proper use of them would be complete without a study of the basic aerodynamics associated with the problem.

Approaches to Sail Shape

There are three different approaches to sail shape, only the last of which concerns us in this chapter.

Naval Architect. A naval architect draws the outline shape of the sails he proposes for the hull he has designed. He must balance the various water and air pressures involved, must study efficiency of rig, and must consider the relevant class or rating rules. I call this *sail outline design*.

Sailmaker. It is the sailmaker's job to give the sails the right characteristics for the conditions in question (strength of wind, boat shape, and type of spars and rigging). This should include selection of cloth, depth and position of camber or belly, and the degree of control to be exercised over the final shape when in use on the boat. I call this *sail flow design*.

Owner. Finally, it is up to you, the owner, to set, trim, and look after your sails so that you get the most efficiency from them through correct shape and angle to the wind. This is *sail handling* in its widest sense.

The job of a sail is to turn the energy of the wind into thrust acting on the boat (which has been so shaped to turn that thrust into forward movement).

Aerodynamics

There are five facts which should be known before this chapter goes any further:

1. When airflow patterns are illustrated the direction and relative speed of the air are shown by the direction and spacing of the lines (called streamlines) which depict the flow: the closer they are together, the faster the flow, and vice versa.

2. When a force acting on a sail is drawn, its power and the direction in which it acts are represented by the length and direction of the arrow. A long arrow means plenty of power, while a shorter one shows weakness. These terms are relative, that is to say that both forces might be called weak by aircraft engine standards, or strong by those of a fly. It is the *relative* power which is illustrated: an arrow twice as long as another represents a force twice as strong.

3. Pressure in a fluid (and air is a fluid) drops as its speed of motion increases; it rises as the speed decreases (this is the famous Bernouilli's Law, which you may hear quoted by the pundits).

4. When fast-moving air (which is at low pressure, as described by Bernouilli's Law) becomes turbulent, as in the stall, it immediately reverts to its original atmospheric pressure.

5. A sharp pressure difference between neighbouring masses of air can only exist if there is some sort of barrier between those masses, such as an aerofoil, a sail, or even a mass of turbulent air.

Airflow Direction

As most of you will know, a boat beating to windward will sail at an angle of about 45° to the true wind. The forward speed of the boat has the effect of making the apparent wind felt on board come from farther ahead. The difference is usually about 15° so, for our purposes, we can assume that the apparent wind angle when close hauled is 30° to the boat's heading. But the sails make an angle of anything from 5° to 20° with the fore-and-aft line of the boat, depending on the sail itself, the weather, and the boat, so they are this much closer to the wind individually. But this is not all. We shall see shortly how the jib and mainsail must always be considered as one aerofoil. If you look at *figure 1*, you will see how a wind of 30° to the boat is at an angle of 10° to the jib, 20° to the mainsail, and 25° to

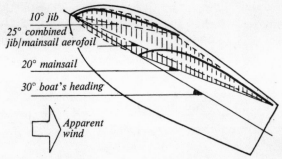

Fig. 1. Apparent Wind Angles. This figure shows the different wind angles relative to different base lines of a boat when beating to windward; the angle made with the boat's heading doesn't vary much from 30° under the more usual close-hauled conditions. The sails, however, can be at finer wind angles, particularly the jib, depending on the angle at which they are sheeted relative to the boat. In the drawing, both mainsail and jib are as wide as they normally ever go when close hauled (10° and 20° to the fore-and-aft line of the boat for mainsail and jib respectively). The shaded portion shows the approximate area of an aerofoil covering both jib and mainsail, and which is at an angle of 25° under these conditions.

the combined jib/mainsail aerofoil of the typical boat shown in the drawing.

Figure 2 shows the general direction and speed of air flowing round an aerofoil placed at an angle of 25° to the main flow. The aerofoil has caused a change in direction of about 10° to the stream-

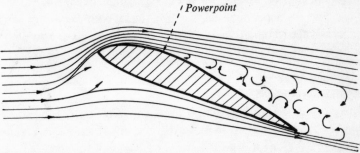

Fig. 2. Airflow Pattern round an Aerofoil. An aerofoil at 25° to the wind. The air is at its lowest pressure on the upper (or leeward) surface just forward of the position of maximum camber (an unwieldy description, which I have simplified by coining the word powerpoint); the closeness of the streamlines near this point reveals their high speed. They break away from the surface just aft of the powerpoint, turbulence sets in, and pressure returns to normal.

11

lines at its trailing edge, and the action of forcing this direction change will result in an equal and opposite reaction (Newton's Law), which takes the form of thrust on the aerofoil.

Figure 3 shows the same conditions around a single sail, shaped like the aerofoil. Note how the slipstreams break away from the lee side of the single sail at about the *powerpoint*; this is the start of the stall, and leeward air pressure reverts to normal in the turbulence aft of this point. I use the word *powerpoint* to describe the position of

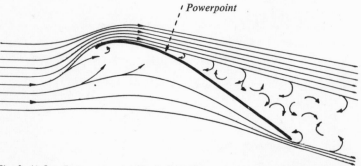

Fig. 3. *Airflow Pattern round a Single Sail.* This typical sail was deliberately drawn a similar shape to the aerofoil in *figure 2.* The powerpoint is about one-third aft from the luff. Well-spaced streamlines to windward mean (relatively) slow airspeed and high pressure; the opposite holds good where they are close together. The flow to leeward is turbulent and inefficient over the after two-thirds of the sail.

maximum camber, because the full phrase is rather cumbersome and I feel that it's about time there was a single word to describe this important aspect of sail shape. Powerpoint seems to me to convey the meaning well, so I shall use it throughout the rest of this book.

Pressure Reduction

There is a difference between the pressures of the air passing above and below an aerofoil, or to leeward and windward of a sail. Mainly because of the way it deflects to leeward from some distance in front of the luff of the sail, the air immediately to leeward has farther to travel to rejoin the air which follows the more direct route to windward. This means that it must go faster to get there in the same time, which in turn means lower pressure to leeward and a tendency for the sail to move from windward to leeward (from high to low pressure).

Pressure Increase

This pressure reduction to leeward is helped by an increase in pressure to windward. The speed of the airflow on the windward side will be slower than that of the leeward flow because it is on the inside of the bend. This difference is heightened by friction on the surface of the sail, which slows down the air to windward more than that to leeward. The slow-speed air to windward will therefore have a higher pressure than normal, and this can be seen in the spacing of the streamlines in *figure 3*.

Impact Effect

This pressure difference is also heightened by impact effect. The force of wind striking any surface acts at right angles to that surface,

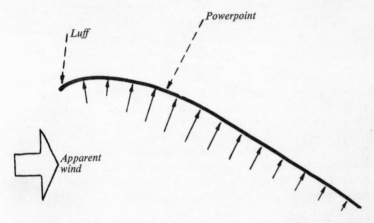

Fig. 4. Impact Effect. The force of the wind striking a sail acts at right angles to the surface. There is some turbulence just aft of the mast, so impact there is reduced; friction slows the wind in immediate contact with the surface as it travels across the sail, so impact is also reduced towards the leech. Maximum impact effect is experienced near the powerpoint.

regardless of the direction of the wind. *Figure 4* shows a typical distribution of this force along the chord of a sail; the longer the arrow the greater the force. The values alter because of local speed variation caused by the aerofoil shape and by the build-up of friction, which slows down the air as it gets towards the leech.

13

Venturi Effect

A venturi is a funnel through which air passes. If it is the right size and shape, it improves the airflow by increasing its speed, lowering its pressure and ironing out turbulence.

A normal venturi is shaped as shown in *figure 5*, but the gap between a mainsail and a jib can also have a similar effect on airflow. This gap is known as the slot, and its shape is of special importance.

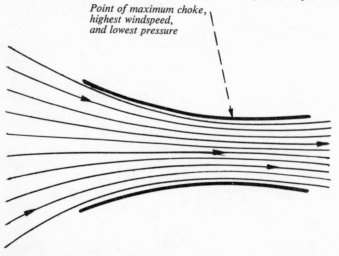

Point of maximum choke, highest windspeed, and lowest pressure

Fig. 5. The Venturi. A typical venturi, such as is used in the working section of a wind tunnel to increase airspeed locally above that of the main stream. This smoothes out the flow and reduces the pressure as the speed increases, and has its application where a jib is placed in front of a mainsail, as we shall see in the next figure.

Figure 6 shows a typical airflow pattern round a well-matched mainsail and jib. Compare it with the flow round the aerofoil in *figure 2*, and note the smoother flow pattern covering more of the lee side of the sails; this means that more of both sails is doing work. The slot also speeds up the airflow to leeward, thus reducing pressure still further to give extra power.

Wind tunnel tests have shown that the leech of the jib should come at least as far aft as the powerpoint of the mainsail, for best advantage to be obtained from the slot. Anything less than this disperses the effect of the slot like a venturi which is too wide, and *figure 7* shows a

Powerpoints

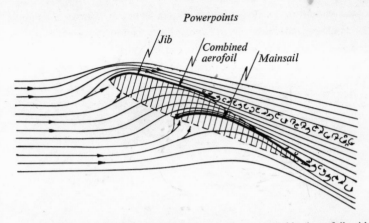

Fig. 6. The Slot. A mainsail and jib must be imagined as one combined aerofoil, with a slot through the middle, and not as two aerofoils with a slot between them. The two sails in this figure form an aerofoil about the same size and shape as the one in *figure 2*. Note how the venturi effect of the slot sees that the flow sticks to the lee side of the mainsail well past its powerpoint, and also draws the air along the lee side of the jib so that it not only stays smooth past the jib powerpoint, but turbulence does not set in until past the powerpoint of the whole combined aerofoil. Compare this leeward flow with that in *figures 2* and *3*.

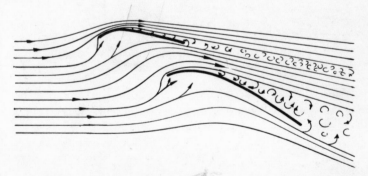

Fig. 7. Slot too open. This slot is too open, because there is neither enough overlap (the leech of the jib should reach nearly to the mainsail powerpoint for best efficiency), nor are the two sails close enough together. Full venturi effect is not obtained because the two sails revert to being individual aerofoils and thus cease to be mutually supporting; the wind speed is allowed to dissipate, and the airflow breaks away from the lee of each sail independently, near its powerpoint.

15

slot which is too open. If, on the other hand, the jib comes too close to the mainsail, blockage and turbulence occur (*figure 8*) and the mainsail will be backwinded. (This often cannot be avoided in the stronger winds, even with the best-shaped sails and venturi, because

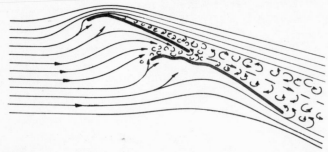

Fig. 8. Slot too narrow. This jib leech is nearly level with the mainsail powerpoint, but it is too close to that sail. Air cannot get through quickly enough to revitalise the leeward flow, and turbulence builds up in the slot. The whole leeward airstream is badly disturbed.

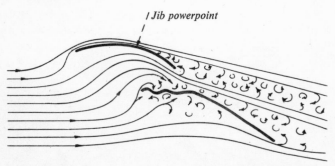

Fig. 9. Backwinding I. The flow of this jib has moved aft over a period of time, through the action of the wind stretching the cloth; the powerpoint is over halfway back from the luff, and the sail is said to have a bellied leech. The airflow off such a jib is directed into the lee of the mainsail, which is backwinded, causing turbulent conditions.

so much air is trying to force its way through the slot.) This will also happen if the leech of the jib curls, either from too much belly (*figure 9*) or from a curled leech tabling (*figure 10*). For best efficiency, the airflow at the exit to the slot should be parallel to the lee side of the mainsail.

16

Total Power

A composite picture of these various forces is given in *figure 11*, where pressure reduction (to leeward) and the sum of pressure increase and impact effect (to windward) are shown by the dotted arrows. For convenience, these forces are usually indicated by a single arrow giving the strength and direction of the total power, which can be said to act through one point on the sail known as the centre of effort; this total power is shown by the solid arrow.

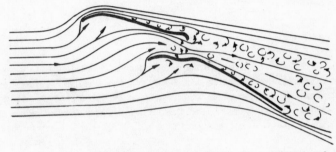

Fig. 10. Backwinding II. This jib has a flat run-off to the wind until the last three or four inches, where the cloth has stretched while the tabling or selvedge at the very edge has held fast. This is the cupped, or 'question mark' leech, and the wind is sharply turned and braked with resulting turbulence and backwinding of the mainsail.

This principle of total power holds good for any normal wing section or aerofoil, and the centre of effort usually ranges a little either side of a point about a quarter of the way back from the front of such an aerofoil, its movement depending on aerofoil shape, angle of attack, and wind strength. Where a jib is hoisted in front of a mainsail, it is important to remember that the two sails combined act as one aerofoil with a slot through it to improve the airflow. The total power of both sails still acts through a point one quarter back from the front of this combined aerofoil—that is to say through the jib. This helps to explain the great importance of the jib.

Resolving the Forces

You will see in *figure 12* how the total power arrow (thin) is pointing at an angle to the direction of movement of the boat, as it was in

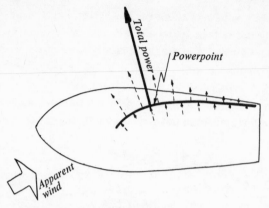

Fig. 11. Total Force. The sum of the windward pressure forces and the leeward suction forces (dotted arrows) can be shown by one (heavy line) arrow. This shows the strength and direction of the total force by its own length and the way it is pointing. When a boat is close hauled, this direction will usually be aft of a line at right-angles to the wind, and forward of right-angles to the boom. It acts through a point known as the centre of effort, which moves about according to wind strength and sail trim, but is usually slightly forward of the powerpoint.

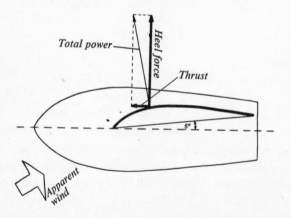

Fig. 12. Thrust and Heeling Forces. The total force in a sail can be divided for theoretical purposes into two forces acting at right-angles to each other (heavy line arrows) in a parallelogram of forces. In a boat sailing to windward the heeling force is usually between four and five times the force thrusting the boat forward.

figure 11. If this total power is resolved mathematically into forward and sideways thrusts (thick arrows), we can then see how much is available to push the boat forward and how much is trying to heel it or drive it sideways. Under close-hauled conditions the forces trying to heel the boat are usually about four and a half times stronger than those driving her forward.

Figure 13 shows the dramatic effect which easing the sheet has on forward thrust (providing the sail stays full). An increase in the boom

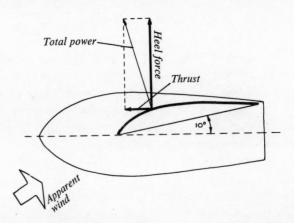

Fig. 13. Effect of Sail Angle on Thrust. Forward thrust varies, for the same total thrust, according to the angle the sail makes with the boat. If the boom is eased from its position in *figure 12*, even by as little as 5°, thrust will immediately be increased by a half, and heeling force slightly decreased. Wind tunnel experiments have shown that the jib is even more sensitive to these changes of angle than the mainsail.

---

angle of no more than 5° adds 50 per cent to forward thrust, and reduces the heeling force a little as well. To increase forward thrust by the same amount without altering the boom angle would mean finding enough extra wind from somewhere to increase the total power in the sail by 50 per cent, and this in turn would increase the heeling force by the same amount.

These are points which you will have to bear in mind when reading the section on trim.

2 Sail Flow Design

I said in the chapter on theory that sail flow design (the decision on how much belly or flow to give a sail and where to put it) is the sphere of the sailmaker, and I implied that it need not concern the owner. This is only true in that you, the owner, can do little to influence the method of achieving a particular shape; you will, however, be better able to get the best from your sails if you know how and why they are made the way they are.

Tailored Flow

One way of building flow into a sail is by adding extra cloth in a convex curve to the luff, in what is called round, so that fullness is increased. *Figure 14* shows a mainsail sewn together and lying on the loft floor before it has had the rope or tape added (which tends to wrinkle the sail and distort the fair curves on the luff and foot). When

Fig. 14. Tailored Flow I. Flow is built into a sail by adding extra cloth in what is called 'round' at the luff and foot.

the sail is roped and then set on straight spars, the round on the luff and foot will be forced back into the sail in the form of fullness, as shown in *figure 15*.

Fig. 15. Tailored Flow II. When the sail is set on straight spars, the extra cloth at luff and foot is forced back into the sail in the form of fullness.

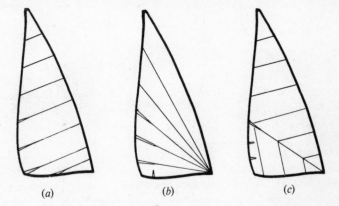

Fig. 16. Broad Seam. Position of tailored flow in a sail can be controlled by tapering the panels from which the sail is made, just as a dressmaker controls the shape of a dress by gussets and tucks. The horizontal cut (*a*) lends itself to this treatment but, where seams are not conveniently placed for this shaping, two half-width cloths may be put in—as shown in the foot of (*a*), or special darts may be inserted, as in the foot of the radial-cut sail in (*b*) or the luff of the mitre-cut sail in (*c*).

Broad Seam

If the sailmaker wants to control the position of this fullness, he will taper the cloths or put in darts in much the same way that a dressmaker controls the shape of the dress she is making. This tapering of cloths is called broad seam, although there are many other words for it, the darts or gussets being variously called seam, nips, or pies among other names.

Figures 16 (*a*), (*b*), and (*c*) show this broad seam put into mainsails of three different cuts, either where two cloths join or as darts specially put in because there is no suitable join in the right place.

Where the mast or forestay has a bend or sag in it, the sail has to be cut to suit. If the mast curves under tension from the kicking strap

Fig. 17. *Allowance for Mast Bend.* If a mast bends in action, it will quickly absorb all the luff round designed to give ·fullness to a sail which has been made for a straight mast. The sail must have extra round built into the luff, according to the amount and position of bend in the mast. This drawing shows in dotted outline the luff of a sail made for a straight mast (shown by long and short dashes) and, in the thin continuous line, the further round needed to accept the curve of the mast (thick line) as drawn, if it is to keep any fullness at all when it bends. If enough cloth is not added for this bend, or if the mast bends more than the sailmaker has been told, then the sail won't fit, and creases will appear from the clew to the point on the luff where the sail is most lacking in extra round.

---

and mainsheet, the mainsail must be cut with extra round to the luff to allow the mast to bow forward; any further luff round for fullness must be added on top of this allowance, as can be seen from *figure 17.*

22

The forestay of all boats sags to some extent, so the jib luff has to be cut with reduced round to allow for this. In addition, a jib should be flat, especially in the head, so that wind is not directed from a full belly into the lee of the mainsail; the upper luff needs to be hollowed further to achieve this. Some flow is given to the lower half of the sail

Fig. 18. Allowance for Forestay Sag. All forestays sag to some extent, so a jib must be cut less full to allow for this shape. The head should be fairly flat and little or no round is needed, but some fullness can be given to the sail lower down, so we get the curve shown in this drawing, where the dotted line represents a theoretically straight forestay.

by rounding the luff but it should not be overdone, for extra flow can always be achieved by easing the sheet; we finally get a shape as in *figure 18.*

Induced Flow

We shall see in the next chapter how synthetic sailcloth is constructed and how it stretches, in common with all other woven materials, when it is subjected to enough strain. While efforts are made to cut this down, some stretch is useful to the sailmaker providing it is not too much and he knows where and how it will appear. By laying his cloths so that lines of tension either come on the threadline or on the bias, he can control the development of flow in different parts of the sail.

The action of pulling the luff of a mainsail until it stretches beyond the length it was made does not make the sail any bigger. If it increases in one measurement it must decrease in another. In this case it is the cross measurement at half height which reduces as the leech roach is pulled towards the mast. The harder you pull, the more the leech will come across, and you will pile up extra cloth just behind the luff, where it will lie in a fold. This shows the flow in the sail, and it will be blown aft again by the action of the wind. If the wind is strong enough to blow this flow well aft to an inefficient position near the leech of the sail, a harder pull on the halyard will

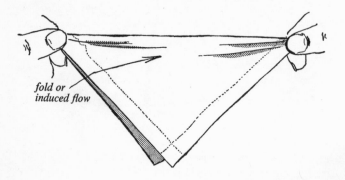

fold or induced flow

Fig. 19. Demonstration of Induced Flow. Fold a clean handkerchief corner to corner, and pull the other two corners away from each other. This will put tension at 45° to the bias of the cloth, and will bring a fold of induced flow along the 'luff' of the handkerchief. The harder you pull, the deeper will be the fold, and the two loose corners will rise as the 'leech' is drawn towards the 'luff'.

draw it forward again. The same holds good to a lesser extent along the foot of a mainsail. You can illustrate this by pulling a handkerchief folded cornerways, as shown in *figure 19*; as you pull harder, so will flow appear as a fold near the 'luff' of the handkerchief, while the free-hanging corners draw in towards the fold, thus reducing the cross measurement.

This movement of flow needs to be controlled. Unrestricted hauling on the halyard and outhaul will cause the luff and foot to stretch too far and may damage the sail. So that this does not occur, a rope or tape is sewn along the edge of the sail with tension carefully graded to allow just the right development of this *induced flow*, as I call it.

24

Jibs. During the first half of this century, jibs were made with wire in the luff to take the strain put upon it by the halyard. This meant that induced flow had to be arbitrarily fixed in each particular sail by the sailmaker, who made the luff of the sail shorter than the wire and then pulled the sail until he had what he felt was the correct tension, whereupon it was fixed to the wire for all time by a seizing. Thousands of jibs are made in this way still, and very good they are too, but recently the benefits have been appreciated of being able to control the luff tension in a jib in the same way as a mainsail. The result has been the adjustable or stretchy luff jib, which I prefer to call by the more positive name of *control luff jib.*

It is usual for a dinghy jib to be made with a wire, rather than a tape or rope, in the luff. A conventional jib is seized all the way along the wire and the sail is given pre-set flow in the luff as described above. A control luff jib is either seized at the head only, or else seized at both ends of the wire and the luff merely sleeved on to the wire so that it 'floats'; an eye is worked into the luff near the tack. The flow is controlled by varying the tension on the luff by pulling down on the eye, which is virtually a Cunningham hole (of which more anon).

The object of altering the tension on the luff of any sail is to vary the amount of induced flow: the more you pull, the more flow will appear at the forward part of the sail. We have already seen that this cannot come from nowhere and in fact comes from the leech as it is drawn forward. This means that less excess cloth is available at the aft end of the sail to be distributed around as flow, so the sail flattens aft.

Thus, when increasing wind drives the flow from the luff towards the leech, it can be drawn forward again by increasing the tension on the control luff.

Camber

A full sail is needed for light weather and a flat one for heavy weather. This is a rule which needs qualification. What is full and what is flat? What about light weather which becomes heavy? Isn't some fullness required in heavy weather; if so, where, and how much? Whereabouts should fullness be in a sail?

How Full? One of the troubles which besets a sailmaker is this question of fullness. What one man thinks is flat may be only medium to another; what is medium to one may be full to someone else. Unless some sort of yardstick is used, you are likely to end with the wrong answer. When ordering new sails, the best way is to compare your needs with another suit for the same class by the same sail-maker, who can then refer to his records and make the new sails flatter or fuller as required. For the purposes of this book we can say that a full mainsail is one which has a depth of belly anything from 15 to 20 per cent (1 in 5 to $6\frac{1}{2}$) of the distance from luff to leech at the point in question (chord). A flat one has a belly of about 5 to 10 per cent (1 in 10 to 20), while the medium sail comes somewhere in between, overlapping rather more at the full end of the scale than at the flat end; see *figure 20.*

Light Winds. If a suit of very full sails is hoisted in light weather, it should do well while the light winds hold. In most waters, however, one of two things usually happens: either the wind dies away, or else it freshens to a medium strength or more. In the first case it won't matter what sails you have, for you probably won't finish the course; in the second case your boat will be knocked down as too much heeling force builds up, as described on page 19. Ultra-light weather sails lose more races than they win.

Heavy Weather. Of greater importance is heavy weather. Gone are the days of really flat sails, made so that the wind could slide off without heeling the boat too much—it also slid off without driving it very much either. Nowadays bendy masts allow fullness to be taken out of the sail (*figure 44*, page 59) as the wind gets up, and the head in particular can be feathered to reduce heel effect aloft, where it hurts most. Sliding seats and trapezes allow crews to hang out far-ther, thus balancing the boat better so wind need not be spilled so much. You will want a fair amount of drive, and there should be anything up to a 10 per cent belly immediately over the boom; this gives power low down where it is most wanted.

Mainsail Fullness—Where? A dinghy which has both mainsail and jib should have a mainsail with the powerpoint between a quarter and

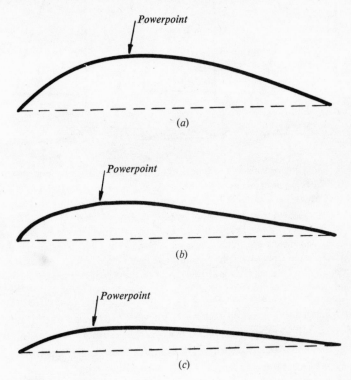

Fig. 20. How Full is Full? The curves in this drawing show the shapes produced by depths of flow at the powerpoint of 17 per cent or 1 in 6 (*a*), 11 per cent or 1 in 9 (*b*), and $7\frac{1}{2}$ per cent or 1 in $13\frac{1}{2}$ (*c*) of the cross measurement; these are typical shapes for light, medium, and heavy weather mainsails respectively. Note how the powerpoint is moved gradually forward as the sail becomes flatter. The shapes are those which the sail should take up when the wind is blowing into it.

a third of the way from the luff towards the leech *when the sail is under the influence of the wind.* This means that a heavy weather sail should start with its flow right forward, for it will blow aft in strong winds; a medium weather sail should allow for some movement of

27

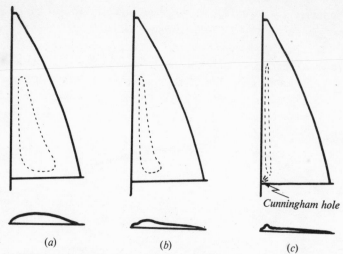

Cunningham hole

(a)   (b)   (c)

Fig. 21. Fullness with the Boat at rest. These curves show the shape of the mainsails drawn in the previous figure, while they are in the dinghy park without the full action of the wind blowing into them. In light weather there will not be enough wind to change the shape of (a) so it should not be hoisted hard enough to draw any of the flow forward; medium weather will cause a slight shift in flow towards the leech, so enough tension is put on the luff to cause the beginnings of a fold to appear (b); the flow which has been induced in the form of a fold up the luff of sail (c) will be blown well aft by heavy weather, so not only should there be plenty of tension on the halyard, but a Cunningham hole should be pulled down if one is fitted.

flow, which should therefore be just forward of the one-third point; flow in a light weather mainsail (if you *must* have one) can be tailored to the one-third position, for there should never be enough wind to blow it anywhere else. *Figures 21 (a), (b),* and *(c)* refer.

Una or Cat Rig. A boat with only one sail, like an OK or a Finn, doesn't have the benefit of a jib. This means that the air will separate from the lee side of the sail at the powerpoint, because there is no slot effect to delay this breaking away. In order to keep the air in contact with the sail as long as possible, so that low pressure to leeward can cover a greater area, this powerpoint is taken aft about halfway towards the leech. If it were put any farther back, the shape of the aerofoil would be reversed and the leech would act as a brake when beating to windward. *Figures 22 (a), (b),* and *(c)* show the reasoning behind this.

28

Jib Fullness—Where? One of the two main functions of the jib is to produce an efficient slot (the other is to carry the main driving force of the combined mainsail/jib aerofoil). For best efficiency, airflow at the exit to the slot should be parallel to the lee side of the mainsail, as we have already seen. This means not only a jib leech which doesn't curl but also one which has a flat run for quite a way into the sail. The flow of a jib should therefore be well forward and the sail should have as flat a leech as possible, with no hook to the extreme leech and no belly in the aft part of the sail (see *figure 6*).

Spinnakers

In all cases other than a dead run the wind flows across a spinnaker from luff to leech. For most of its life, therefore, it acts like a large jib, but without the benefit of the latter's straight luff and flat leech. The chief danger in designing the flow of a spinnaker lies in the upper half of the sail. If you try and get too much cloth into the head, you will end with such a deep belly (often called a Roman nose) that there is a permanent pocket of dead air which disturbs the even flow across the sail, setting up turbulence (*figure 64*, page 90). Besides being better on a reach, a moderately flat head will make the sail better in heavy weather, as it will have less knock-down effect than a full sail.

Dinghy spinnakers usually have tapes on the leeches. It is important that these are strong enough, do not shrink, and even stretch a little with the cloth. If they cause the edges of the sail to curl (possibly from the cloth stretching slightly while the tapes do not), you will get an inefficient shape, particularly on a reach (*figure 81*, page 124).

If you want extra area in your spinnaker, one way it can often be safely added is by means of a skirt at the foot. This is extra round built on to the foot and is sometimes allowed by the rules. It has the advantage that it does not risk the Roman nose problem I mentioned above, so the airflow remains virtually undisturbed; equally the additional weight of cloth doesn't have to be lifted so high by the wind, so it is more likely to set properly in light airs. If your boat is a slow mover downwind in Force 2, it's worth talking it over with your sailmaker.

29

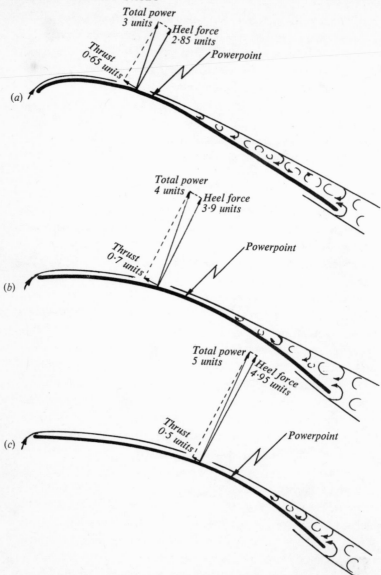

Total power
3 units
Heel force
2·85 units
Powerpoint
Thrust
0·65 units
(a)

Total power
4 units
Heel force
3·9 units
Powerpoint
Thrust
0·7 units
(b)

Total power
5 units
Heel force
4·95 units
Powerpoint
Thrust
0·5 units
Powerpoint
(c)

Fig. 22. Powerpoint Position in Cat Rig. Where a mainsail operates without a jib to smooth out the airflow to leeward, turbulence sets in just aft of the powerpoint. In a cat-rigged boat such as the Finn, therefore, it is logical to have the powerpoint rather farther aft than usual, in order to delay airflow separation and thus get more of the sail doing useful work. Sail (*a*) is a conventional sloop's mainsail with the power-

30

point one-third aft. Its total force, without the help of its jib, measures 3 units, and the forward thrust is 0·65 units. The powerpoint in the cat-rig sail at (b) has been put farther aft to the midway position, with the result that the total force in the sail is increased by about one-third to nearly 4 units for the same conditions, because separation of the airflow from the lee side of the sail is delayed by shifting the powerpoint aft, thus more of the sail is doing useful work. Although the direction of this force is angled slightly farther aft, thus reducing the proportion available as forward thrust, the actual driving power is increased by about 10 per cent over sail (a) to 0·7 units; but note that the heel force has also gone up by rather more.

If we now take the powerpoint even farther aft in order to make more of the sail work to increase the total force still more, the direction of this force is by now angled so far aft that the forward thrust component is reduced to 0·5 units, or 25 per cent below that of sail (a); in addition, the heel force is by now nearly double that of sail (a).

In practice it is found that sail (b), with its powerpoint at the midway position, is best for cat-rigged boats.

3 Sailmaking

It is the object of this chapter to tell you something of what happens in a loft when a sail is made. It is not possible to cover the subject more than superficially in 19 pages: it takes nearly half that many *years* to become a sailmaker. But a background knowledge will be useful in looking after your sails.

Sailcloth

First comes sailcloth. Almost exclusively, jibs and mainsails are now made of synthetic polyester cloth; this is called by its trade names of Terylene in England, Dacron in America, and a variety of other titles all over the world. It is all made to the same chemical formula, invented in England in 1941; any difference in the finished cloth lies in the way the raw material is woven and then subsequently treated.

Terylene, Dacron, or whatever you like to call it, is virtually immune from the effects of water and from a wide variety of chemicals, although it can suffer if bits of dirt or salt work their way into the weave and then chafe the threads; in addition, mildew can form on it if damp and dirt are also present (as it can on glass under similar circumstances); finally, prolonged sunlight or industrial smoke (constant exposure for a year or so) can weaken the material to the point where it will tear like paper. When woven into cloth it is strong, doesn't stretch a lot, doesn't soak up water, and can be woven close enough to be smooth and pretty airtight. The ideal sailcloth, you might say—and you wouldn't be far wrong.

A good deal depends on the way the threads are woven into cloth. If they are slackly arranged on the loom and not banged up tightly

32

together at each pass of the shuttle, the resulting weave will be loose, porous, and stretchy. The aim is a firm cloth, which is woven under great tension with the weft, or cross threads, banged close up together as it builds up on the warp, or lengthwise, threads.

Even the highest tension on the most modern looms cannot get the weave tight enough to be all right without further treatment. Therefore cloth straight from the loom goes through a finishing stage. During this, it is scoured and dried, may have chemical or resin fillers added to reduce stretch or make the cloth harder, and is then heat-relaxed to shrink and settle the material, thus helping the individual threads to lock together. Addition of resins can turn a slack cloth into one which has a pleasing appearance for a time, but they break down in use and become detached from the cloth, to run off with rain or spray in a milky liquid, or else the surface deteriorates into typical marble crazing as the filler cracks. This process of build-up and break-down can be likened to starching a shirt or blouse.

Improved weaving techniques, pioneered and spurred on by Ted Hood of America, have led the way to achieving sailcloth which is so closely woven under great tension that little or no added chemicals are needed, and the only finishing process is heat relaxation. This is the ideal, for there are then no fillers to break down and the cloth does not deteriorate so much with use; such a cloth is also much softer to the touch than one which is heavily resinated. Its main drawbacks are that it is more difficult to sew without puckers, and light sails are liable to wrinkles; therefore cloth destined for dinghy sails often has a hardener added. The sailcloth with which we are mainly concerned thus has some kind of chemical added in the finishing stage and is none the worse for it. Technical advances in recent years have been such that these chemicals stick to the weave much better, and there is so little of them that only a small proportion of cloth is below standard in this respect.

Recent research in England by ICI Fibres Ltd has revealed more about the way in which synthetic cloth stretches when it is made into sails. This in turn indicates a requirement for different cloth construction, depending on how it is going to be used. Stretch in the head of a horizontally cut mainsail, for instance, is partly across the cloth, whereas it is more along the run of the warp nearer the foot: this points to cloths of different warp and weft construction being needed for the top and bottom of a mainsail. A mitre cut jib, on the other hand, stretches more across the cloth than along it, so a relatively heavy weft construction is advisable. Variation of cut (radial, vertical, spider-web, etc.) will alter the direction of local stresses in the cloth and will change the requirement.

Apart from these considerations, it is sometimes a good idea to use a stiff cloth for the upper half of a mainsail to help support a large roach, while the foot is made of softer material to encourage the development of flow.

All this, of course, goes on outside your control. What can you do about cloth? Tests which you can make to prove the quality of sailcloth which you are being offered are twofold.

Stretch. Pull a sample between your hands at an angle of 45° to the weave (the angle of least resistance to stretch). You will produce a small fold in the material (induced flow), depending on the strength you use and the quality of the cloth. This fold should recover when you stop pulling, and the more it recovers the better the cloth. You will become a better judge with practice, so compare one or two cloths before pronouncing judgement.

Fillers. Crumple a sample of cloth and then rub it back and forth between your hands as though washing it. You will soon see if there is a lot of loose filling in the material, for it will craze and possibly even flake off if it is bad.

One of the most important factors in sailcloth, as I implied above, is its resistance to stretch (in the jargon of today it is said to need a high modulus of extensibility). Any woven material will stretch if tension is applied on the bias (at an angle to the threadline), and sailcloth is no exception. Indeed some stretch is useful, as we have already seen in the previous chapter: it enables the sailmaker to influence the amount and position of flow in the sail. Bias stretch shows movement of the weave. As pull is exerted at an angle to the threadlines, so the little squares formed by the weave distort into little diamonds (*figure 23*). This causes the material to get longer in the direction of pull, but as it does not get any bigger the extra length has to come from somewhere, and the cloth shrinks across the line of the pull. Translated into terms of a sail, a pull on the luff acting at an angle to the threadline (which usually meets the luff at an angle)

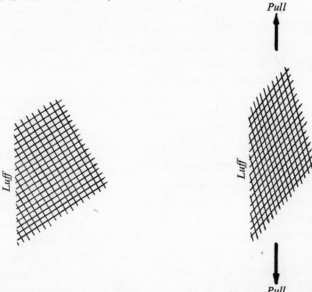

Fig. 23. Bias Stretch. Woven cloth will stretch at an angle to the threadlines, because the little squares formed by the weave will distort into little diamonds; if the pull is along the threadline, either warp or weft, no such distortion takes place and stretch is almost eliminated. For this reason most sails have cloths at the leech (where stretch would be bad) laid so that the threadline runs in the same direction as the pull—along the leech. This usually results in the cloth meeting the luff on the bias, where movement of the weave can be used to induce flow in the sail. Note how stretching the luff brings the leech across, thus reducing the cross measurement. This shows that you can't get something for nothing, i.e. the sail doesn't get any bigger when the luff and foot are stretched—it merely distorts the original area to a different shape.

causes the luff to grow longer but the leech to pull over towards the luff, thus reducing the cross measurement of the sail.

'Plated' Cloth. Sometimes a sailmaker will recommend a particularly heavy cloth (200 to 250 gm/m²) which has a hard finish, where a dinghy has a sail plan which will profit from this. An example is the British Merlin Rocket, which can get more area aloft if a stiff cloth is

used to help hold out a top batten which becomes almost a free-standing gaff. In this case the sail relies almost entirely on tailored flow for its shape, because the cloth won't stretch as easily as a soft material and so won't form the fold up the luff which is induced flow. So-called plated cloth has two main drawbacks: creasing and insensitivity. Extra care has to be taken to stop the heavy finish from cracking and creasing, and so making the sail inefficient. Also, a jib made of hard cloth will not give advance warning of the stall by quivering up the luff as the boat points too high; this can be overcome by a tell-tale sewn into the luff of the jib, if you are one of those who can work to windward while using it without getting hypnotised!

Cloth Weight. In England sailcloth is measured by the number of ounces it weighs to each square yard. In America the width of cloth to be measured is fixed at $28\frac{1}{2}$ in (an Old English standard for broadcloth) and the ounces in every yard of this rather narrower material are weighed; this results in a figure lower by some 20 per cent than in England for exactly the same cloth. When grading a particular piece of cloth, therefore, you have to weigh more actual material under the British system than you do under the American, and this is well illustrated in *figure 24*. Countries using the metric system weigh the number of grammes per square metre, and this is the method I use in this book because it can only mean one thing. I have given a comparative scale for all three systems in *figure 25*, and you can see that a normal dinghy weight of material for a mainsail and jib of $4\frac{1}{2}$ ounces per square yard (oz/yd²) in England, is equivalent to just over $3\frac{1}{2}$ ounces per American yard (oz/yd × $28\frac{1}{2}$ in) and 150 grammes per square metre (gm/m²) on the Continent.

Mainsail Cuts
A sailmaker has to be careful how he lays the cloths of his sail. Tension directly on the line of the threads—either lengthwise (warp) or crosswise (weft)—will not result in much stretch, as no distortion of the little squares formed by the weave will occur. As soon as the angle of pull comes off the threadline, even by as little as 1° or 2°, stretch starts to take place and must be allowed for.

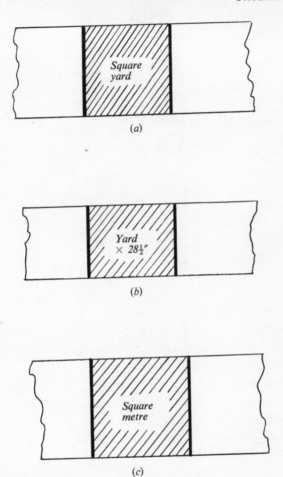

(a)

(b)

(c)

Fig. 24. Cloth Weight Measurement. Imagine two rolls of sailcloth, one of which is 36 in wide and the other 28½ in wide. If a yard length of each of these otherwise identical cloths is cut off and weighed, the wider cloth will have a larger area (a) and will tip the scales at a greater weight than the narrow strip (b). Sailcloth in Great Britain is weighed in yard lengths of 36-in-wide material (36 × 36 in); in USA the standard is a yard length of 28½-in-wide material (36 × 28½); 28½ in is an Old English broadcloth standard somehow inherited by the Americans from the days of Robin Hood. There is thus less material to be weighed in America, and the apparent difference between the two systems when describing the same cloth is about 20 per cent.

The metric system measures grammes per square metre (c).

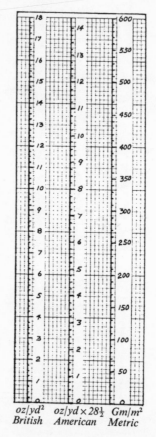

oz/yd²	*oz/yd × 28½*	*Gm/m²*
British	**American**	**Metric**

Fig. 25. Cloth Weight Conversion Table. In America sailcloth is graded by the number of ounces in a yard of cloth 28½ in wide (oz/yd × 28½); in Great Britain it is ounces per square yard (oz/yd²); countries using the metric system weigh the number of grammes in a square metre (gm/m²). This table converts from one system to another at a glance.

This explains why a mainsail is usually made with cloths running at right angles to the leech, so that pull in this unsupported area will be kept on the line of the weft or cross threads (*figure 26*). With a conventional horizontal cut, cloths meet the luff at an angle, ready to receive the tension of the main halyard on the bias and to produce a fold along the lines of that tension if it is great enough; this is one way of inducing flow in a sail and we have already seen the use made of it.

Fig. 26. Horizontal-cut Mainsail. The most conventional mainsail cut is horizontal. This brings the weft (or cross threads) parallel with the stress lines which follow the curve of the leech—particularly if the cloths are overlapped slightly more at the luff end, so as to trip them round the perimeter of the leech. The cloths reach both foot and luff on an angle, so that the material will stretch and give induced flow fairly easily. Finally, there are plenty of cloth joins in the right places to put in broad seam to help the process of shaping.

Both the horizontal and mitre cut mainsail respond to the above theory (*figures 26* and *27*). Other cuts are vertical (*figure 28*) and radial (*figure 29*), neither of which would appear to have much resistance to stretch in the unsupported leech, particularly where a curved leech means a constantly changing bias angle. A way of overcoming this latter problem is to fit small panels in the leech, with the threadline (usually weft) parallel with the leech as shown in *figure 30*.

To overcome the drawback of lack of stretch in the lower luff, due to the low bias angle of radial sails in that area, some sailmakers combine it with the vertical cut to produce a semi-radial cut as shown

39

Fig. 27. Mitre-cut Mainsail. A mitre-cut mainsail has the same advantages as a horizontal cut, plus the fact that more cloths strike the foot, so that broad seam can be better incorporated to tailor the flow. The drawback of this cut is that the mitre itself, being double thickness, may be rather hard and slow to stretch. If this happens, it can stop the clew drawing aft, to the detriment of flow development.

Fig. 28. Vertical-cut Mainsail. This cut suffers from changing bias at the leech, as the curve of the roach cuts across the threadlines; I have drawn typical warp and weft threads in various cloths in order to show how these meet the edges. Its chief merit would appear to be that of novelty.

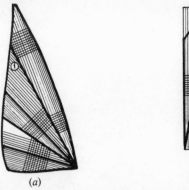

(a)   (b)

Fig. 29. Radial-cut Mainsail. Like the vertical-cut mainsail, the radial or sunray cut suffers from bias stretch along the leech. In addition, luff bias changes from a large angle aloft to nearly nothing near the tack, which results in uneven stretching of the luff, with less give in the lower half than above halfway (the reverse of what is wanted). There is also different bias stretch at the seams: if the panels are economically cut two to a cloth as shown in 29 (b) alongside, then there will be bias joined to bias at one seam, and selvedge to selvedge at the next.

The main advantage claimed for the radial cut is a better absorption of the stresses in the sail, which radiate from the clew. But the disadvantages of uneven stretching, both at the leech and the seams, would seem to me to outweigh this gain.

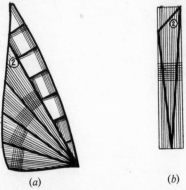

(a)   (b)

Fig. 30. Radial Cross-cut Mainsail. This version of the radial cut has short lengths of cloth laid at the leech as for a horizontally cut sail, to bring the threadline on to the line of the pull round the curve of the roach. In addition, the radial panels are cut with the warp threadline running down the middle, and not along one side as a selvedge. Both sides of the panel, therefore, have similar bias and similar stretch characteristics; all radial seams will thus stretch the same. This is more expensive on cloth, as only one panel can be taken from each length of material.

41

Fig. 31. Semi-radial-cut Mainsail. One of the disadvantages of the radial cut is the lack of stretch ·in the lower luff, where the panels meet the luff nearly on the threadline; this is particularly bad where a Cunningham hole is used. To overcome this, the lower cloths can be laid at approximately 45° to the luff, and running full width as for a vertical cut sail.

(a)

(b)

Fig. 32. Mitre-cut Jib. Standard mitre-cut jibs have the weft threads parallel with both leech and foot, to keep down stretch in these highly stressed areas unsupported by rope, tape, or wire. The mitre, apart from being just another seam to offer the risk of wrinkles, is extra thick and so resists stretch; it can produce a hard line of unstretched material.

Synthetic cloth, however, has enabled sailmakers to allow the foot a certain amount of bias, so that it will stretch a little (b). This helps the mitre to stretch, lets the clew draw aft and allows the flow of the sail to develop, thus giving a flat run-off to the leech.

in *figure 31*. This is claimed to give most of the advantages and few of the disadvantages of both cuts, but the sail now seems to be unduly complicated and I still suspect the leech.

Jib Cuts

Where cut is concerned, the same basic rules as for mainsails apply to jibs. The big difference in the case of the jib is that the sail has two unsupported edges (leech and foot), so it is important to have the weave lined up on both these sides if stretch is to be eliminated; this leads to the mitre cut which we all know (*figure 32*). The drawback of this cut lies in the mitre itself. It is thicker than the rest of the sail, and so tends to stop the full development of stretch along its line.

In order to let the clew draw aft and thus flatten the leech, it is a good idea to let the foot of the sail stretch a bit. This means that the cloths should leave the foot at an angle (anything from 2° to 15°), and the mitre cut sail sometimes has the foot cloths deliberately offset a bit as in *figure 32 (b)*.

Other cuts which take advantage of the fact that the cloths in the foot don't nowadays have to be on the threadline are the horizontal

Fig. 33. *Horizontal-cut Jib.* There is no mitre in a horizontal jib and this means that not only is there less work involved in making the sail (thus keeping the price down) but there is less doubled cloth to stop the clew drawing aft to flatten the leech. As I have said before, stretch along the threadline (as opposed to on the bias) is almost nil in sailcloth. Between warp and weft, there is slightly less stretch on the latter because the threads across the cloth are already under greater tension than those lengthways (due to the mechanics of weaving). This almost complete absence of stretch, however, when coupled with the danger of sewing the leech seams tightly, means that there is a slight danger of a hooked leech with this cut.

and the vertical (*figures 33* and *34*). They both do away with the restricting influence of the mitre, are simple to make and result in good sails. The vertical cut jib is possibly superior to the horizontal for dinghies because it has a seam-free leech, which is more important to keep flat than the foot. If the leech is cut fairly straight (i.e. without hollow) and heat-sealed instead of having a tabling, then the chances of a curling leech with this cut are few.

Fig. 34. Vertical-cut Jib. The vertical jib is another way of getting simplicity of cut. The leech is uncluttered with seams and, if this is heat-sealed instead of having a tabling, it is remarkably clean and free from curl. The vertical cut can be used instead of the mitre cut for dinghy jibs with advantage.

Another cut is the spider web (*figure 35*), but the object of this is to keep down stretch in any part of the sail by reducing the run of the cloth before it comes up against a seam. It is therefore more suited to large sails where the stresses are great, and is not suitable for dinghy sails where cloth lengths are never very great anyway.

The radial cut jib (*figure 36*) is the last with which we need concern ourselves. It suffers from the same problems as a radial mainsail, with the particular disadvantage of different bias angles at each panel in the luff, which means different stretch and thus different amounts of induced flow up the luff. You may also get uneven stretching between individual panels in the sail unless the cloths are cut to their wedge shape by trimming equally from each side, as shown in *figure 30* for the mainsail.

Fig. 35. Spider Web Jib. This cut reduces the size of each piece of cloth in the sail. The result is that stretch anywhere in the sail is kept to a minimum, so that the cut is best suited to large jibs with specially heavy loadings; it is not recommended for dinghy jibs as it restricts development of flow in small sails. Disadvantages are that there are several different bias angles at the luff, so stretch will be uneven; also the doubled cloth at each mitre will stop the clew drawing aft to flatten the leech in all but the largest sails.

Fig. 36. Radial or Sunray Jib. This type of jib suffers from the same disadvantages of changing and different bias stretch as a radial mainsail. A jib's leech, however, is usually straighter than a mainsail's, so threadline problems in this area are less. But a jib relies for its flow more than a mainsail on stretching the luff, so the different bias angles in this area will bring even more problems than in a mainsail.

45

Putting Together

It is no good having a good sail perfectly designed and cut if the machinist who puts it all together can't sew carefully and consistently. A seam which wanders off line, even for a few inches, will start wrinkles at best, and cause hard spots and major creases at worst. The sewing machine is a vital link in the chain of sailmaking, and a good operator is worth almost as much to a sailmaker as is a good hand worker for finishing off the sail with cringles, casing, slides, and eyelets.

Tablings

The unsupported edges of a sail (the leech of a mainsail, leech and foot of a jib) are subject to stresses due to the pull of sheets, wind pressure, and boom weight. Such an edge, in dressmaking, has a hem to reinforce it, and it can also have one in sailmaking, where it is called a tabling.

Fig. 37. Cupped Leech. If the leech tabling is too wide and strong, it may stretch less than the sail just inside, or forward, of it, which will result in a hollow or cup just at the leech, in the shape of a question mark. This causes backwinding and 'motorboating', which is such a destroyer of morale, and is a good reason for heat-sealing the leech without any tabling at all.

The width and weight of tabling on a sail can make a big difference to the set of a sail: a narrow tabling might allow too much stretch to the leech; a wide one is stronger and stops the leech stretching at the very edge but, if the sail just forward of the tabling stretches, you get a cupped or question mark leech (*figure 37*). The sailmaker will decide the width and strength of tabling according to the task of the sail, and then lay his cloths at a corresponding angle to the leech so that it stretches just the right amount: narrow tabling and no bias angle for a light sail; wider tabling and a bit of bias (say 1° or 2°) to

46

allow it to stretch a bit, tabling and all, for a general-purpose sail. It's a good idea to do away with the tabling altogether at the leech of some racing jibs, and to seal it with a hot soldering iron in order to fuse the threads together on the raw edge to stop them fraying. This gives a clean run-off to the air, and so means a better airflow along the lee side of the mainsail. Such a jib has a shorter life than one with a tabling because, not only does the sail tend to fray at the leech (it can be resealed but the process cannot go on indefinitely), but the unreinforced leech is vulnerable to mishandling and is quick to stretch out of shape.

Luff Rope or Tape

A mainsail has to have a rope on the luff to enable it to slide up the mast groove. Sometimes this rope has a second job whereby it controls development of induced flow in the luff of the sail, while in other sails the luff is controlled by a Terylene or Dacron tape and the rope is fed inside this tape, where it acts as a safety precaution to prevent overstretching.

The advantage of having a tape on the luff is that the sailmaker is dealing with similar materials both for the sail and for the luff control. In addition there are no seams in a tape, as there are in a tabling, to chafe on the mast groove and pick up splinters from wooden spars.

Ancillary Items

Your sailmaker will be the best one to help you finalise your decision on ancillary items and extras. He will certainly have his own ways and reasons for doing many of the tasks set out below, and will be pleased to talk them over with you. If his ideas are not what you are expecting, he will take a deal of persuading that your way (or mine, for that matter) is better than the one he has been following successfully for a good many years. You would be unwise to try and talk him into a new technique without being prepared for the worst consequences.

Headboard. For years dinghies used to have wooden headboards sewn through holes in the board into pockets at the head of the mainsail. These proved too cumbersome and heavy aloft so were abandoned in favour of alloy, but the system of hand-sewing through holes in the board was a constant source of creases in synthetic cloth. There are now several ways of stiffening the head of a mainsail including sewing through an alloy board as before, slipping the board into a pocket where it remains loose and free from stitching actually through it, or riveting a plastic board on one or both sides of the sail outside the cloth. The aim is to keep creasing and weight to a minimum.

Window. A window in a sail is allowed by most rules nowadays and is a first-class extra if it is put in right. Even if it only reveals one boat on starboard tack during its lifetime, it will have repaid its original cost. Being made of a material which bends but does not distort or stretch, it should be placed in a fairly flat part of the sail, otherwise it will have to try and take up complex multiple curves and will thus make creases. It should also be sewn on to the sail before the cloth is cut away, so that it lies evenly over the area and does not pull at one corner after the canvas is cut away. If you have fixed ideas of window position, it is best to order a new sail without one, try it out afloat, and then mark the sail exactly where you want it to go. Most class rules limit the size of windows, and many prohibit them being nearer to the leech or foot than a certain distance (usually about 6 in); this is to stop extra thick windows being fitted to act as battens supporting a large free roach area.

Zippers. A zipper may be fitted along the foot of a mainsail to close off extra fullness in the sail, either in the form of a slab reef or a shelf (which is really only an extreme form of the same thing). Both are useful additions to thrust when reaching and running (I did some wind-tunnel tests on the shelf foot as fitted to an International 14-ft dinghy, and unzipping it on a reach with everything else unaltered produced 5 per cent more forward thrust) and they can also help windward work when unzipped in light weather. The idea of closing the zipper is to flatten the sail for windward work in anything but the lightest winds (*figure 38*). Similar zippers may be fitted up the luff, but they are usually more trouble than they are worth for it is often

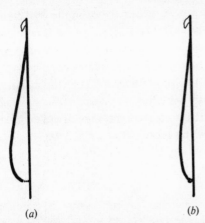

(a)   (b)

Fig. 38. Zipped Shelf. These two drawings show the principle of the shelf foot, which can be closed off by means of a zipper to make the sail into a more normal shape (*b*). The shelf is unzipped when the boat comes off the wind (*a*), increasing forward thrust by as much as 5 per cent. Depending on its depth, it may also be unzipped when close hauled in very light weather.

Care should be taken to see that the sail is not too flat when the zipper is closed, because it is just over the boom that fullness is most useful.

impossible to reach the slider if it jams. It is not practical to fit a zipper after a sail has been made because the extra cloth which it controls is not built into the foot; if you want one, therefore, it should be specified when a new sail is ordered.

Cunningham Hole. I shall go into greater detail on Cunningham holes in the chapter on trim. It is enough here to say that one can very easily be put in after the sail is made, and its cheapness and efficiency make it a Best Buy.

Battens. Battens may be made of wood, plastic, or glass fibre. Their job is to help spread and support the roach, usually at the leech of a mainsail, although some jibs have them in either leech or foot. They should be stiff enough to stop the roach from flapping, but should bend enough to take up the natural curve of the sail. This means that the inner end should be thinner than the leech end and a top mainsail batten should bend rather more than the rest; plastic is often chosen for the top batten for this reason. If a batten goes right across to the

49

luff of the sail, its length, tension when in the pocket, and amount of bend must all be right if it is to set properly. If only the top batten is full length it should lie in its pocket with very little tension because, if it is held in hard enough to force it into a curve, it may refuse to bend the other way when you change tacks in light winds. Full-length battens lower down the sail don't give this trouble so much and their tension can be varied to control the amount of flow in the sail. It is to enable you to vary this tension that full-length battens usually tie into the sail, rather than slip into pockets with a pre-set elastic tensioner at the inner end.

Jib Foot Round. Some rules do not control the amount of round on the foot of the jib and this can offer a way of increasing area by a significant amount. Even a narrow jib with a short foot can have up to 10 to 12 in of round built on to it if a stiff cloth is used or a drawstring is fitted to help hold it in shape. This certainly pays off when reaching and it can also be made to set when beating to windward if the boat is sailed right; see description of power sailing on page 83.

4 Rigging and Tuning

We are concerned with sails, but the mast and rigging help the sails work well or badly, so we must take a close look at them too.

Mast Function

A mast has two jobs. First, it must hold the sails aloft; secondly, it controls the belly of the mainsail. To do the first it needs to be strong enough, with supporting rigging where necessary, to stand up to the pressures it will meet from wind in the sails. To do the second it must be able to bend in a controlled manner so as to flatten the mainsail by the right amount, in the right place, at the right time.

Mast Construction

Mast Shape. It is not my intention to go in detail into the construction of masts as such, but they exert a great influence over the airflow round a mainsail and so a few words are needed. A square mast which doesn't rotate and so is always at an angle to the wind creates most turbulence. You may be surprised that a so-called streamlined shape which doesn't rotate also causes a lot of disturbance; if the mast is fixed, a near round section is better (*figure 39*). A pear-shaped mast which swivels into the wind is better again, and if it rotates past the dead upwind angle it is better still. One which is wing-shaped is best of all, but these are unwieldy and are liable to be blown over in the dinghy park; they are specialist items with which specialist craft are concerned, and are not allowed by most conventional dinghy classes. To sum up, if your mast is fixed, have a section which is nearly round; if it rotates, have a pear-shaped section and turn it rather more than into the wind for best efficiency.

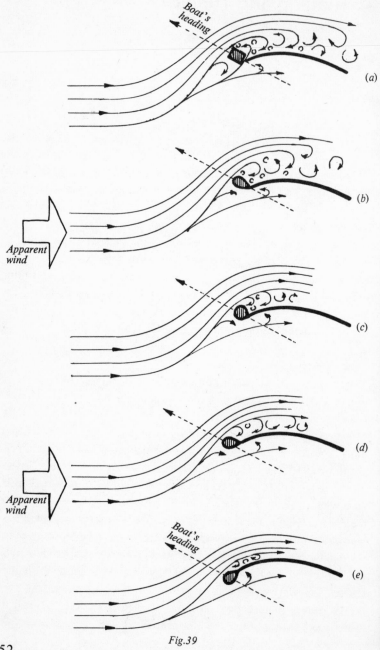

Fig.39

Drag. There is a lot of drag put up by shrouds, diamond wires, jumpers, spreaders, and so on. Therefore, a mast which does away with some of these will be a better streamlined shape than one with a lot of wires and struts. Bottlescrews and terminals cause more air eddies than plain wire so it also pays to bury them inside the mast if possible; otherwise they only add to the amount of unnecessary ironmongery presented to the wind, which should be kept to the minimum safe and efficient level.

Note that I have qualified the safe minimum level by adding the words 'and efficient'. It's nearly as bad to have a mast which is not properly stayed and braced, and so bends wrongly, as it is to have one which breaks.

Bendy Spars

The basic aim of bendy spars is to flatten the mainsail. They also have a number of other effects such as easing the leech and opening the slot, as we shall see shortly.

The main force which bends a mast (and boom) is tension applied by means of the main sheet; the kicking strap can also impart bend on certain occasions, although when it is most needed (when going to windward) you will nearly always find that the mainsheet pulls the boom so far down that the kicking strap hangs loose.

Fig. 39. Mast Streamline. A square mast, which is at an angle to the wind, causes a lot of disturbance to the airflow (*a*). If the sail is attached to the mast by slides running on an open track, there will be a loss of thrust due to the leak of pressure to leeward through the gap between the luff and the mast.

Most racing dinghies have a streamlined mast with a groove for the bolt rope (*b*); this causes less disturbance and seals the gap between sail and mast. But a non-rotating pear-shaped mast always presents an unstreamlined shape to the airflow except when the boat is head to wind; a round section (*c*) offers less wind resistance. If class rules allow, and the mast will rotate into wind, disturbance of the air is even lower (*d*). Because of the way the wind bends to leeward just before it reaches the mast (see earlier drawings showing general airflow patterns), the mast should be turned some 15° past the direction of apparent wind (*e*) for best results when close hauled; it can then actively help the airflow take up a smooth path by becoming in effect a mini-wingsail.

Clutter, in the form of wires, spreaders, jumpers, etc., should be kept to a minimum to reduce drag.

Flattening. When a mast bends it bows forward in the middle, thus taking out some of the round built into the luff of the sail to give it fullness. A glance back at *figure 17* will show how this luff round is absorbed by the curve of the mast, thereby flattening the sail. The same process takes place with a bendy boom, as shown in *figure 40*, but fullness along the foot gives efficient thrust low down, so the sail

Fig. 40. Boom Bend. In the same way that a bending mast flattens the sail up the luff, so a bending boom will flatten it long the foot, in the shaded area of this drawing. This does not affect the overall fullness of the sail as much as the bending mast but, as it is low down and in front of their very eyes, it is readily noticeable by the crew; this tends to make it a popular refinement. It is just over the boom, however, that fullness gives best efficiency, for it has little effect on heel so low down, but gives plenty of forward thrust. When you add the fact that a bending boom also tends to make the mainsail leech go slack (which can, however, be cured by use of a Cunningham hole), this item is not necessarily an essential part of 'go-fast' equipment.

shouldn't be flattened too much in this area. You need to start the process near the head, where heel force is greatest and forward thrust least. The sail can then be progressively flattened towards the foot as the wind gets stronger, in order to get rid of power in excess of that which you can control.

Leech. As well as altering the fullness of the mainsail, bendy spars affect the leech. When a sheet pulls down on the end of a stiff boom against a stiff mast, tension is added to the leech which gets tighter. When the pull is applied to the middle of a bendy boom fitted to a bendy mast, the ends of the boom bend up, the mast head comes aft and tension is eased along the whole leech area. The most obvious symptom of this is a crease running from the clew to the inner end of the bottom battens: this can be cured by pulling down on a Cunningham hole to increase tension in the sail.

Slot Opening. When the mainsail is flattened the slot will get wider as the mainsail powerpoint is drawn away from the jib. In addition, thrust along a boom acting on a bendy mast not only pushes it forward but also to windward, because the boom is angled off to leeward (*figure 41*). This causes the mast to bow slightly to windward and carry the mainsail bodily away from the jib, thus also helping to open the slot. A wider slot allows more air to pass through it undisturbed, which is what we want in stronger winds.

Control of Mast Bend

It is not enough for a mast just to bend. You must be able to control the amount and position of bend if you want to make the most of it. This depends on:

1. The material the mast is made of.
2. The shape and thickness of the mast section.
3. The shape of the sail.
4. The controls used to limit bend.

Material. A wooden mast can be made to bend more than a metal one but, size for size, it will not be as strong. If you pay a lot of money for it, you can get one which might be lighter than a metal mast, with a lower centre of gravity (which all helps to make it easier to keep the boat upright when it is blowing hard). But besides being more expensive to maintain, it may be affected by hot sun or water absorption or it may bend in unexpected places and amounts, whereas a metal mast will be more predictable, will go on bending the same way year in and year out, and will possibly have a smaller area to present to the wind (because it is stronger and so can be made of a

55

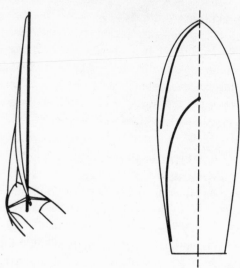

Fig. 41 (a). Mast Bend and the Slot I. When the mast is straight and the sail therefore has a lot of camber, the slot is fairly narrow because the jib leech is near the lee side of the mainsail at its powerpoint.

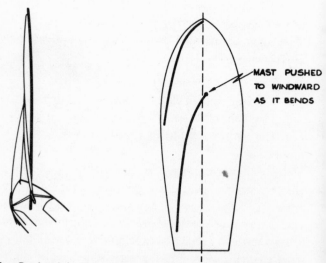

Fig. 41 (b). Mast Bend and the Slot II. When the mast is bent in order to flatten the sail, the lee side of the mainsail is drawn away from the leech of the jib. In addition, the act of bending the mast forces it slightly to windward, thus opening the slot still farther. This is fortunate, because it occurs in higher wind speeds, which need a wider slot so that more air can pass through it.

56

smaller cross-section). On the whole a metal mast is best for most racing dinghies.

Section. There are various different sized cross-sections available for metal spars, which all have known bending characteristics; you can thus choose the basic flexibility of your rig fairly accurately. The bend of a wooden mast can be altered by shaving it down where you want more bend, but this can't be carried on indefinitely without dangerously weakening it. It is unusual for two wooden masts to bend exactly alike, whereas it is possible to be pretty certain how a metal mast of given section will behave under most conditions.

Sail. If a sail is cut without much round to the luff, a bendy mast will soon absorb all the spare cloth available, and it will then be stopped

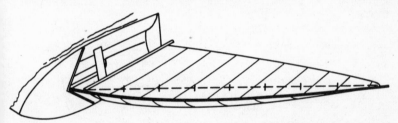

Fig. 42. Measuring Mast Bend. Hoist a mainsail which will allow the mast to bend the right amount, tighten the kicking strap normally, then lay the boat on her side and haul in the main sheet until the mast is bent as you want it. Stretch a tape measure straight between the tack and the head, and measure the distances (called offsets) from the tape to the mast at 3 ft intervals. Write down the answers or you will forget, and also note whether you start measuring your 3 ft intervals from the head or the tack.

It is important to set a sail which has been made for a bendy mast, or it won't allow a proper curve to be taken up. If you don't have a suitable sail, you can get a fair result by attaching the main halyard to the outer end of the boom to give the right leech length, and then pulling down on the main sheet as before.

from bending any more by the tensions in the sail. The lesson here is that mast and sail must be matched if they are to perform well together. You must tell your sailmaker how much your mast bends before he makes you a new mainsail; he will then cut it to fit. *Figure 42* shows how to measure the bend on a dinghy mast.

57

Controls. You can control the bend in any particular mast in four main ways: mast chocks (a screw crank, or a piston controlled by means of a line working through pulleys or on a drum is more complicated but more effective), rigging, main sheet, and kicking strap.

Chocks. Every stayed mast has two fixed points through which it must pass at all times: the heel and the hounds. A mast which is stepped in the bottom of the boat (rather than on deck) and which

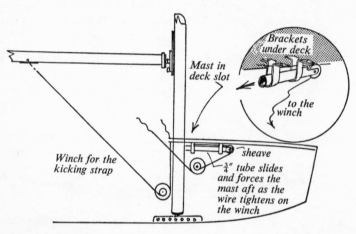

Fig. 43. Control of Mast Bend at Deck Level. If you use a chock to control mast bend at deck level, you will probably find that you won't alter it a lot while sailing, because you are most likely to want to vary the bend as the wind increases, and it is not always possible to change chocks in heavy weather. The system shown here has the advantage that it is simple to operate, and is therefore more likely to be used. A screw crank, or worm gear, would also do the job, but would take longer to adjust.

passes through a gate is also restricted in its movement at deck level by the play allowed by the slot in the deck. If a chock or other form of adjustable control (*figure 43*) is used to limit fore and aft travel, mast bend will be limited; sideways bend is usually restricted by the width of the gate. A look at *figure 44* will show how a mast which is not allowed to bow forward at deck level bends aft from the top only, whereas one which is free to bend as it wishes will bend evenly all the way up. Thus, if you only want to flatten the top of the sail you

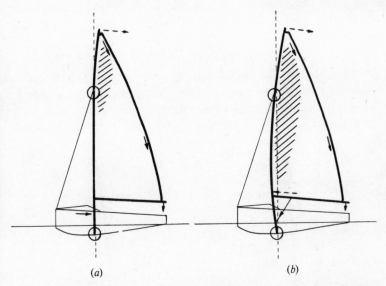

(a)   (b)

Fig. 44. Flattening by Mast Bend. Most of the forward thrust in a mainsail comes from the lower half of the sail, and most of the heel force from the upper half where sideways moment is greatest. As the wind increases and heels the boat more, the mainsail should be flattened progressively from the head down. This feathers the sail, and is shown shaded in the drawings. In this way as little forward thrust as possible is lost, while heel force is reduced according to the crew's ability to keep the boat upright.

A mast is normally anchored at the two points circled in (a) and (b): the heel and the forestay attachment. Depending on the material and section of the mast, and its arrangement of stays, it can be bent by pulling hard down on the main sheet. If a stop is placed in front of the mast at or near deck level (see *figure 43*), it will not be able to bow forward below the forestay, and bend will be restricted to the mast head only, thus flattening the sail in that area; see *44 (a)*. When further flattening is wanted, the stop is removed, or eased, thus allowing the lower half of the mast to bow forward and take cloth out of the middle of the sail; see *44 (b)*.

A deck-stepped mast acts all the time like one which goes to the bottom of the boat without a stop to hold the lower half straight. Bend is controlled by tension on the main sheet (and, to a lesser extent, on the kicking strap), and by the arrangement of stays; see *figures 45 to 49*.

59

should stop the mast moving forward in the gate; if you want to flatten the whole sail you should remove the chocks (or allow the crank or piston to go forward) and allow the mast to bow forward at deck level.

Jumpers. Jumper stays will also control bend at the top of the mast. *Figure 45* shows how jumpers which are tight will keep a straight mast head, while slackening them off allows it to bend back. Any

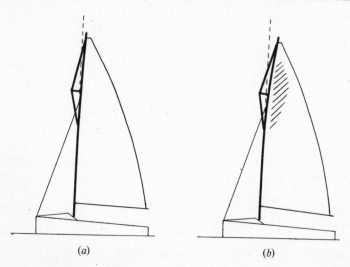

(a)   (b)

Fig. 45. Jumper Stays. Tight jumper stays as in (a) mean that the mast head is stopped from bending back. When the jumpers are eased off as in (b), the mast head is free to bend more, thereby flattening the sail in the head. More or less the same effect can be produced by chocking the mast at deck level as in *figure 44 (a)*, without the damaging wind resistance produced by jumpers.

unnecessary weight and windage aloft is a handicap you can well do without, however, and you want to think twice before you start making your mast look like a radar aerial; about the only time when jumpers may pay is if there is a lot of unsupported mast above the hounds, such as on the 14-ft International.

Spreaders. In the absence of diamond shrouds, spreaders are chiefly responsible for control of the sideways bend of a given mast section. They achieve this largely through their length, and *figures 46, 47,*

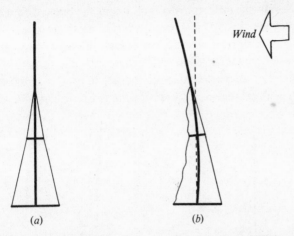

Wind

(a)   (b)

Fig. 46. Lateral Mast Bend—Short Spreaders. Short spreaders which do not reach as far as the shrouds pull the shrouds inwards when the boat is at rest (*a*). As the lee shroud goes slack when close hauled, the windward spreader pulls the mast to weather at that point (*b*). The amount by which the spreader is short is only an inch or so, and both this and the bend of the mast have been exaggerated in the drawing.

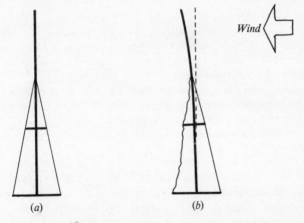

Wind

(a)   (b)

Fig. 47. Lateral Mast Bend—Even Spreaders. Spreaders which just reach the shrouds, so that they are neither pushed out nor pulled in when the boat is at rest, give fairly good support in light airs (*a*). As the wind increases, the amount of mast movement will depend on how the rigging is set up in the first place: tight shrouds will let the mast bend from the spreaders upwards; slack shrouds will let it lean to leeward as well as bend (*b*). Here again, the amount of bend has been exaggerated in the drawing to make it easier to see what is happening.

61

and *48* show the different effects of spreaders which, with the boat at rest, pull the shrouds inboard, lie evenly on them without tension, and displace them outboard. The actual differences we are talking about are only measured in half inches, so I have had to exaggerate the drawings. A displacement of about ½ in to 1 in outboard is the most usual arrangement, and spreaders with adjustable ends are

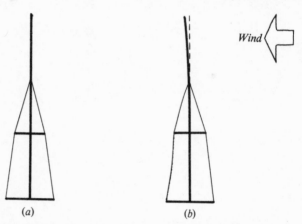

Fig. 48. Lateral Mast Bend—Long Spreaders. Spreaders which push the shrouds outboard of the straight line by an inch or thereabouts will give most support (*a*). If the rigging is set up hard, the mast will stand up to quite a lot of wind before it bends much to leeward (through the wire stretching), except above the hounds (*b*). The drawing is exaggerated for clarity.

Spreaders where you can adjust the length are useful, because they not only let you tune shroud displacement through a range of 2 or 3 in, but change in mast rake also alters the position of the shrouds in relation to the ends of the spreaders; if you alter mast rake, you must also alter spreader length if you want to keep mast bend the same.

worth having, particularly as their length has to change with mast rake if shroud displacement is to remain the same. Fixed spreaders also affect fore and aft bend, as can be seen from *figure 49*, and some boats use fixed spreaders which also displace the shrouds slightly forward when the rig is at rest, so that there is a tendency to pull the middle of the mast aft even before there is any wind in the sails: when the mast wants to bend, the fixed spreaders will restrict bend. Swinging spreaders, on the other hand, allow the mast to take up its curve without setting up any cross-tensions in the rig and they also allow the leeward spreader to swing forward out of the way of the sail when the boat is running; this not only allows a better shape but also cuts down chafe. The best of both worlds can be had by having spreaders which will swing forward to cut down sail chafe, but which won't swing back (and so will help restrict mast bend if that is what you

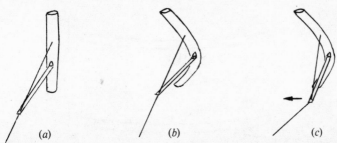

(a)   *(b)*   *(c)*

Fig. 49. Fore-and-aft Bend—Swinging and Fixed Spreaders. When the mast bends out of the straight line (*a*), it causes the spreaders to move forwards at their inner ends in relation to the shrouds; see (*b*) and (*c*). Swinging spreaders (*b*) allow the angle to vary, and thus avoid awkward cross tensions building up in the rigging. Fixed spreaders (*c*) cause the shrouds to be displaced forward of their line, thus setting up a pull aft, which restricts mast bend, because it is pulling the centre of the mast aft against the bend.

want). Careful study of spreaders and shroud tensions can help do away with the need for diamonds and jumpers even on the lightest mast sections and still keep bend within controlled limits.

Main Sheet. The pull of the main sheet is transmitted through the leech of the mainsail to the mast head causing it to bend back, as shown in *figure 44.* The effect of the sheet differs according to where the pull is applied to the boom (on the outer end or in the middle) and also, to a lesser extent, on the arrangement of the blocks. *Figure 50 (c)* shows how sheet tension which is angled forward applies more thrust along the boom to help push the mast forward in a bend low down. Less forward thrust bends the mast higher up.

Kicking Strap. While a kicking strap does not have such leverage on the boom as a main sheet, it acts at an angle of about 45° to the boom and so exerts a forward thrust as well as its downward pull; it thus has some effect on mast bend. You will find, however, that the

63

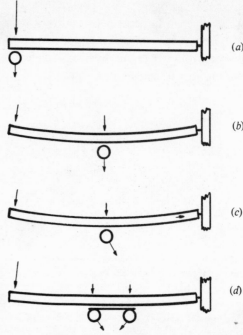

Fig. 50. Main Sheet Leverage. (*a*) Pull on the outer end of the boom will have most leverage down the leech of the mainsail, and least along the boom. This will bend the mast high up, and leave the boom straight (the latter may even bend upwards in the middle, due to the pull of the sail, and thus increase fullness in the foot). (*b*) A centre-boom attachment which leads vertically down splits the pull between bending the mast and the boom. (*c*) If the sheet leads slightly forward from the point of attachment to the boom, a proportion of the pull will be along the boom, thus helping to push the mast forward at the gooseneck and bend it low down. (*d*) If the attachment is divided and spread over a wide enough distance, the boom will bend less and put more tension on the leech than it will with a single-point central pull. In practice, it is seldom that the two pullies can be separated enough to make a great deal of difference.

kicking strap usually hangs loose when beating to windward in a stiff blow, showing the more powerful effect on the boom of the main sheet when it is pulled hard down. The kicking strap will tighten as the main sheet is eased on a reach and you should beware of having it so tight that it bends the mast too much; ease it to allow the mast to straighten a bit and give the sail more fullness, but keep it tight enough to keep down twist.

64

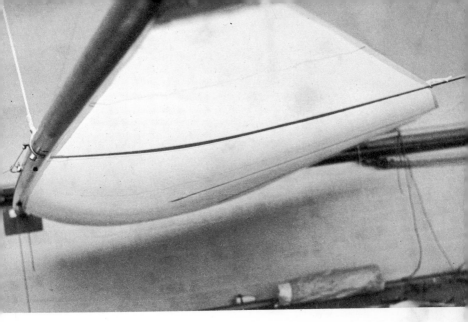

1. A horizontal test rig allows the sailmaker to examine closely all parts of the sail. Here a 505 mainsail is on Bruce Banks Sails' bendy spar. *Yachting World*

2. Several dinghy sails can usually be cut alongside a bigger sail at a large sail loft such as W. G. Lucas & Son. *Wright & Logan*

3. This half-size 18 foot National spinnaker model in Ratsey & Lapthorn's wind tunnel shows all the usual signs of narrowness as seen from your own boat, until . . .

4. . . . seen from ahead. It then appears as the high-bosomed bursting beauty which everyone else's spinnaker always seems. *Bek*

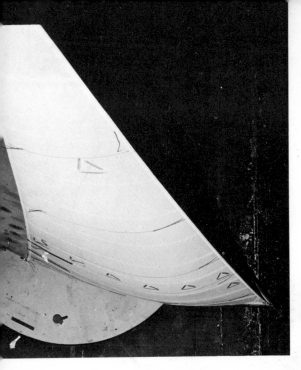

5. Triangles marked on a jib under sailcloth evaluation at Southampton University reveal canvas stretch under load. Note the tufts showing local wind direction. *Yendell*

6. ICI Fibres Ltd of England carries out its own research into sailcloth. This plotter is analysing stereophotographs of full-size sails under load on test spars. *ICI Fibres Ltd*

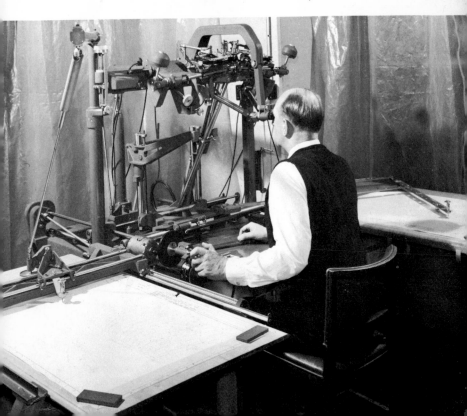

7. A 14 foot Internatio
mainsail on a test rig,
showing the extra belly
given by an unzipped s
(in black). *Howard-
Williams*

8. A model of the same
in the wind tunnel, with
shelf closed off by the
zipper. This resulted in
per cent loss of thrust c
reach. *Beken*

9. Seahorse Sails test porosity with a Gurley meter, which measures the time taken for air to pass through sailcloth of a specific area. *Seahorse Sails Ltd*

10. A mast slot with variable stops. Note a[l] the adjustment lever o[n] starboard shroud in th[e] background, and the use of jam and Clamcleats. *Gina Hu[n]*

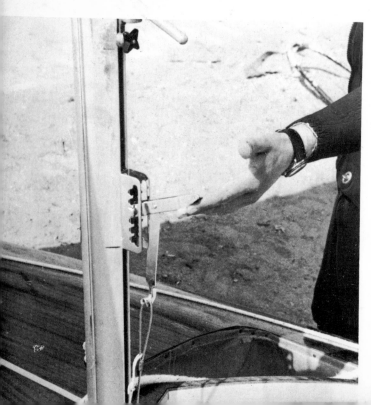

11. Jib halyard tension lever. The halyard is wi[re] and setting the lever at [the] same stop every time ensures the same tensio[n in] the jib luff every time it [is] hoisted. *Howard-Willia[ms]*

12. A jib roller operated through an endless loop under tension by shockcord. This gives positive control in either direction, and does away with the need to go forward and unwind an obstinately twisted luffwire. *RWO Ltd*

13. Full spar and sail control means having a lot of ropes and cleats. This is all right if the layout is not complicated, and you know how to work it. *Gina Hunt*

14. Clamcleats with no moving parts can be relied on not to go wrong. *Gina Hunt*

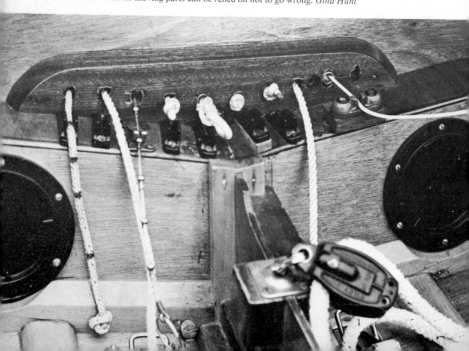

15. Boom bend can take fullness out of the foot of the mainsail. But don't overdo it, or you will lose drive where you want it most — low down. *John Oakeley*

16. A full-width mainsheet traveller, like this one on Britain's 1968 gold medal winning *Superdocious*, coupled with large low-friction blocks, is one of the most important sail-controls. *KH Publicity*

17. A Finn sail with three tack eyes for better control of the flow. *Howard-Williams*

18. This Enterprise mainsail has been hoisted with a slack luff for light weather. *Howard-Williams*

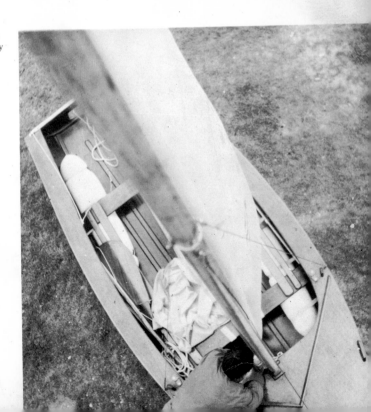

19. Putting more tension on the luff draws the belly forward and flattens the sail. *Howard-Williams*

20. This 505 mainsail appears to be made of light cloth which has stretched too much. It could do with a Cunningham hole in the luff, and a bit more tension on the foot. *Yachts and Yachting*

21. This OK mast is bending too much for the sail, which has not had enough round built into the luff. Mast and sail must always be matched. *Yachts and Yachting*

22. A 14 foot International mainsail showing the typical crease up the inner end of the battens brought on by too much leech roach. *Yachts and Yachting*

23. *Superdocious* showing a beautifully set mainsail, with twist eliminated through correct use of a full width centre-boom traveller. Note the deep section boom to avoid bending this spar. *Eileen Ramsay*

24. This 505 spinnaker pole is hoisted very high which would disengage from the jib if this were as well. The spinnaker pulling sideways a lot, my guess is that the boat astern is catching up; s certainly isn't heeling a much as the leader. *Eile Ramsay*

25. The leeward Fireball has a well-setting mainsail, while the weather boat is sheeted amidships and showing quite a lot of twist. *Howard-Williams*

Precautions

Always remember that it is no good having a bendy mast and all the gear if you have forgotten to tell your sailmaker about it. The sail must be tailored to the mast (or vice versa) for good results.

Mast Rake

Another area where rigging can have a marked effect on performance is in mast rake and the change it brings about in the balance of the boat. The naval architect usually designs his boat to have a little weather helm when it is slightly heeled in medium winds with the

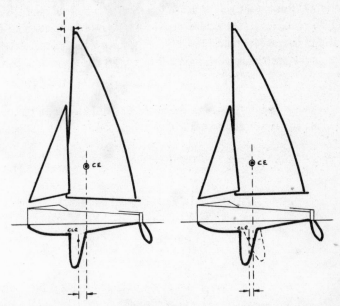

Fig. 51. Mast Rake and Balance. The amount by which the centre of lateral resistance of the hull, centreboard, and rudder (CLR) is forward of the centre of effort of the sails (CE) is called the lead, and determines the amount of weather helm needed to overcome the turning moment and keep straight. These two drawings show in simplified form how the centre of effort moves in relation to the centre of lateral resistance as the mast is raked; this movement is greater if the mast is stepped farther aft or forward by moving the heel. If the mast of this particular dinghy were raked forward of vertical, and the centreboard pivoted aft, a situation would soon be reached where the centre of effort was in front of the centre of lateral resistance. This would need lee helm to hold the boat straight, instead of the more usual weather helm.

centreboard down. That is to say, the boat will tend to turn into wind if left to steer herself. This gives what is known as feel to the tiller and also ensures that any inattention by the helmsman means that the boat makes ground to windward rather than loses it to leeward.

To give a boat weather helm it is necessary for the centre of effort of the sails to be behind the centre of lateral resistance of the hull (including centreboard and rudder). This will have the effect of weather-cocking the boat into wind unless the rudder is held slightly over to one side to counterbalance the tendency. The effect which mast rake has on this carefully balanced system of forces can be seen from *figure 51*. Raking aft will increase weather helm and raking forward will decrease it, as the centre of effort is moved in relation to the centre of lateral resistance. Equally, movement of the centre of resistance as the centreboard is pivoted fore and aft has a similar effect.

Slack Rig

It is a fact that most dinghies go better to windward with the mast raked aft and better downwind with it raked forward. These opposing

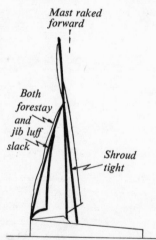

Fig. 52. Slack Rig—Running. The wind has blown the mast as far forward as the shrouds will let it go. The forestay and jib luff are slack, but the jib doesn't mind a slack luff off the wind unless the boat is on a close reach. In this case, you have either got to accept some jib inefficiency, or else have adjustable shrouds to rake the mast aft and tighten the jib luff (because the main sheet is not tight enough to do the job as it does when beating to windward).

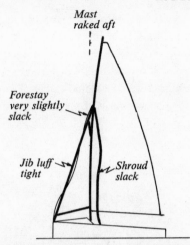

Fig. 53. Slack Rig—Close Hauled. When beating to windward, the mast is pulled back by tension on the main sheet, until it is as far aft as the jib luff will let it go (or, if it is shorter—and it shouldn't be—the forestay). The resulting loose shrouds will allow the mast to lean to leeward, unless you have some sort of adjustment to take up the slack in the weather shroud.

requirements can both be met if the rigging of the boat is slack enough to allow the mast to move back and forth. *Figure 52* shows the mast allowed to rake forward until checked by the main shrouds. This results in a slack forestay, but the jib is not interfered with in its performance under these conditions; indeed, it can use the extra fullness which such a slack stay gives it. In many cases the jib is lowered and a spinnaker hoisted instead.

Figure 53 shows the same dinghy beating to windward. Tension on the main sheet (transmitted through the mainsail leech) has pulled the mast back until it can go no farther due to the limit imposed by the jib luff, which is therefore pulled nice and straight, as required for close-hauled work. Both shrouds are relatively slack, so the one to windward will have to be tightened by means of an adjustment lever of the type shown in *figure 54.* Closing this lever ensures that the shroud is tight enough to stop the mast leaning sideways. Further tension on the main sheet now serves only to bend the mast, as we have seen earlier in this chapter.

Slack rigging and adjustable shrouds are not suited to all conditions. River sailing places greater importance on the anticipation of wind shifts and less on looking into the boat to fiddle with gear for what, in any event, may only be a short leg of the course. Equally, estuary sailing makes it of doubtful value because the slam of a boat in a seaway will soon upset a mast which is not fairly tightly rigged. Nevertheless, there are plenty of occasions when it pays off and its correct setting and adjustment is one of the basic aspects of tuning.

Fig. 54. Shroud Adjustment Lever. There are several ways of adjusting shroud tension quickly, and this Proctor quadrant lever is one. It gives a total throw of $1\frac{1}{4}$ in with six different positions, and the linkage plates have holes for further adjustment. Other systems on the market use the Highfield lever principle. When running before the wind in light weather, both leeward and windward levers are released to allow the mast to go forward and the boom to square off to its maximum distance. In medium conditions the leeward shroud only is slackened; while in heavy weather it is usually wisest to have both shrouds tight. Besides helping to control the mast, use of these levers means that the sail does not chafe on the shrouds so much when reaching.

Jib Halyard

It is no use tuning your dinghy to achieve the mast rake and movement you want if you spoil it all by hoisting your jib as hard as it will go, thus pulling the mast right forward against the stops. A jib luff tighter than the forestay will stop the mast raking aft as much as the forestay would otherwise let it; one which is slacker than the forestay means that the jib luff will hang away from the stay in loops when you are close hauled, which is inefficient. Ideally, you should hoist the jib every time so that the wire luff is *just* tighter than the forestay when beating to windward, as drawn in *figure 53*. This means that the weight will come on the jib when the mast is pulled hard aft in the close-hauled condition, so that then the luff is good and taut. Equally, you will not hold the mast too far forward by overhauling on the halyard. To ensure that this desirable state of affairs is exactly right each time the jib is hoisted you should use a non-stretch wire halyard with an eye spliced in the end to fit a tensioning lever hook on the mast when the sail is up (*figure 55*).

Fig. 55. Halyard Tension Lever. In order that the jib shall be hoisted to exactly the same tension each time (with the luff wire just taking the weight off the forestay), something along the lines of this Racing Dinghy Equipment Company 'Tradewind' lever is required. The halyard has a rope tail to pull down an eye at the end of the wire, which hooks on to one of the lugs and the lever is then snapped home. The throw can be adjusted to either 1 or 2 in, while the arm carries three equispaced halyard supports. Other similar levers are on the market, and one example is shown in photograph 6 (b). 11.

Jib Sheet Leads

A final point of tuning which should receive careful attention is the position of the jib sheet; sometimes this is fixed by the class rules, but often there is a choice.

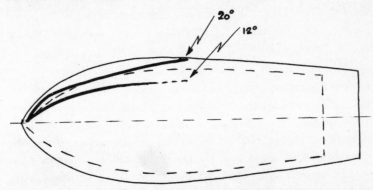

Fig. 56. Jib Sheet Angle I. When viewed from above, the jib should usually make an angle somewhere between 12° and 20° from the centreline of the boat. The smallest of these angles is usually only used by slim, tender boats sailing on smooth waters (although there are exceptions, such as racing scows like the Fireball, which sometimes go down to 12° to 13° even on open water); the largest value is common on bluff, sturdy dinghies sailing habitually on open waters.

When measuring the angle on your deck, remember that 1 in of sideways movement across the boat, 5 ft back from the jib tack, is 1°.

As seen from above, the jib sheet should make an angle of 12° to 20° with the centreline of the boat (*figure 56*). It is impossible to set the limits any closer in a book which tries to cover all racing dinghies, and the exact figure will depend on the shape of the boat, the shape of the sail, and on the sailing conditions.

Boat Shape. A slim, tender, racing dinghy can usually afford to have its jib sheeted to a narrower angle than a boat which is bluff bowed and fairly beamy. This is because the former will normally be more responsive to the tiller and can change direction quickly enough to take advantage of the higher pointing which the finer angle offers. A more chunky dinghy needs to be driven along harder; you could say that there needs to be more brute force and less finesse. Boats of the scow type seem to like the narrow end of the range, even keeping their jibs sheeted fairly hard on a reach.

Jib Shape. A tall narrow jib will have its leech some way from the lee of the mainsail, however close the sheeting angle. This means that a wide angle would be wrong for such a sail because it would open the slot too much. On the other hand, a wide low-cut jib will backwind the mainsail easily and its leech needs to be kept as far away from it as possible, so it should have a wide sheeting angle.

Sailing Conditions. Rough water and blustery winds mean that the slot should be wide enough to pass a lot of air or there will be a poor flow due to blockage and turbulence: the sheeting angle should be wide. In addition, a boat should normally be driven fairly free under these conditions and a wide jib angle helps this requirement. Conversely, smooth water and light winds mean that a narrow sheeting angle can be used to its full advantage.

Fore and Aft Position. Viewed from abeam, the sheet of a medium-shaped jib (i.e. one not cut with a foot particularly low like a genoa, nor particularly high like a cutter's jib) should prolong forward approximately along the line which bisects the clew of the sail; this bisector is sometimes shown by the mitre. A lower sail should have a

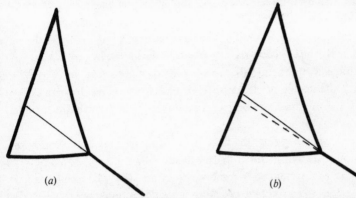

Fig. 57. Jib Sheet Angle II. The angle of the jib sheet, when viewed from beside the boat, depends largely on the shape of the sail. A genoa type sail (i.e. one with a relatively long foot) should sheet with the pull more along the foot than the leech, and a prolongation forward of the sheet should make an angle of about 5° below a line bisecting the clew (*b*). As the foot shortens relative to the leech, so the pull of the sheet should be farther forward, until it is roughly equal along leech and foot for a conventionally shaped dinghy working jib as shown in (*a*); this means that prolonging the sheet forward more or less bisects the clew. The aim should be to arrange tension on leech and foot so that the former doesn't vibrate and the latter has a decent amount of flow in it, yet the leech isn't tight nor the foot slack.

lead farther aft, and a higher one should have it farther forward (*figure 57*).

Active Tuning

Even if you don't achieve anything spectacular by tuning, you certainly get to know your boat and this in itself must result in better performance. Don't forget, it's only a few seconds improvement that we are seeking, so don't expect startling results.

The best way to set about tuning a dinghy is to decide first where you want to step your mast, how much bend and rake you want to allow it, and how slack or tight you are going to have your rigging.

These factors all vary from one boat to the next, let alone between classes. Short of being an expert in the matter you will probably decide what you want by talking to other owners and by examining boats which are known to be fast. Remember that one factor often has a vital bearing on another, so it is no good doing only half of

71

what the fleet leader does and still expecting the same results. A bendy mast needs a sail cut to suit; a whippy topmast needs slack jumpers, or none at all, if it is to be allowed to bend and make the sail flat in the head; slack rigging requires shroud adjusters; a mast well forward in the boat will probably need a good deal of rake aft to bring the centre of effort back, or else a centreboard which is well forward to adjust the centre of lateral resistance so that there is no danger of lee helm.

Having fixed these, the next thing is to go sailing in the conditions you are tuning for. Get a friend to sail alongside you in a dinghy of similar performance, preferably one of the same class and rigged in the same way as your own. Now settle down on a beat to windward and see which boat is going faster. The slower boat should try alterations until she catches up or passes the other (if this never happens, cast a critical eye over the whole boat to see whether some major component is below standard: sails, rudder, centreboard, or surface finish). Then try another alteration and see its effect, each taking it in turn to try something different and, if it proves successful, the other boat making the same alteration. It is important only to try one alteration at a time, or you won't know what is causing any improvement (or deterioration, as the case may be). It is also wise to write down what you are doing so that you will know exactly what to undo if it is not successful, or what to do to the other boat if it works (how many turns of the bottlescrew, how many holes in the adjustment plate, etc.). This is a slow process of trial and error which brings best results to the methodical and persevering owner.

5 Trim

Trim is different from tune in that tune is the basic arrangement and setting up of the hull, mast and rigging, and is best done before the boat ever leaves the dinghy park, while trim is active adjustment of the sails during sailing.

For some owners, however, trim does start ashore with the choice of the right sails: heavy weather or general purpose. But the object of the various controls we have just been looking at is to make one sail able to suit a wide range of wind strengths. We shall now look at some more ways of doing the same thing, and by the end of this chapter I think you will agree that one sail can cover most conditions if the right controls are properly used. The expense of the controls is more than offset by the saving on sails.

If there is a choice of sails it is more likely to be between old and new. In any event, you must now hoist them. The mainsail will usually be made fast to the halyard at the head by a shackle and to the boom at the tack by a pin; if the tack is fastened by a shackle, a common fault is to have one which is too short in the jaws so that the tack eye has to be forced over on to its side in order for it to squeeze into the small space available. This causes distortion of the sail and can lead to creases, and can also mean delay in getting afloat as you struggle with it. For some reason the right shackles seem hard to come by, but it's worth persevering with such a basic requirement until you get what you want.

It is important to see that the clew is properly fastened. A great many dinghies use a lashing at the mainsail clew and while this is cheap, positive, and allows choice of tension, it is almost impossible to adjust while sailing for it takes both hands and all your concentration just when these are most needed to keep the boat going properly. If you do have this arrangement it is likely that your boom is a wooden one of several seasons' standing with a worn groove, so it is important to see that the sail can't pull out of the boom: take a couple of turns round the boom as well as out to its end when you tie the clew lashing.

It is better to have a snug groove and to shackle an outhaul wire direct to the clew so that it can be controlled while sailing. There are various ways of making this outhaul wire adjustable in use, it being better to have a length of rope operating through a system of pulleys inside the boom and coming out near the mast (so it can be adjusted by the crew whatever the boom angle), rather than a handle working on a worm gear at the outer end of the boom (which can only be reached when the sail and boom are close hauled, under stress, near the centreline of the boat, and only then by the helmsman standing up and facing aft).

Main Halyard

It is better to have a main halyard which hooks on to a lug or hook on the mast or perhaps engages a lock aloft when the sail is right up to its upper black band than to have a rope halyard which might stretch and let the sail down, or even a wire halyard with a rope tail on to a cleat, which will never get the sail up to the same place twice. A hook or a lock is positive and easy and leaves adjustment of tension on the luff to the gooseneck slide, which can be raised and lowered on the mast to suit the weather.

A mainsail should always be hoisted with regard to the strength of the wind it is going to meet. We are trying to achieve a sail which will have its powerpoint about one-third of the way back from the luff *when it is under the influence of the wind*. We have already seen how tension on the luff of a sail draws its belly forward and how action of the wind blows it aft again, so we should hoist hard enough to put the flow in a position from where it will move to the one-third point when under way.

Light Airs. In light airs there should be practically no tension on the luff at all (with the gooseneck as much as 2 to 3 in short of the fully stretched position if the sail is an old one or normally on the flat side) so that the sail naturally takes up the nice camber the sailmaker has built into it. The wind will not be strong enough to alter the shape of the sail, so it should start off properly cambered, ready to turn the softest breeze into motive power (*figure 21 (a)*, page 28).

Medium Winds. In medium weather (force $2\frac{1}{2}$ to 4) the mainsail should be hoisted hard enough to draw the flow forward into a fold up the luff of the sail; it will blow back from there as soon as you start sailing. This normally means that the sail has to be right out to its black bands, but some slightly undersized sails may still be half an inch or so short of their marks, particularly at the lower end of the wind range (*figure 21 (b)*).

Heavy Weather. In heavy weather the sail should be pulled right out, and the Cunningham hole drawn down if one is fitted. It is important to get the utmost tension on the boltrope or tape, for the strong winds will blow the camber right aft to an inefficient position if given half a chance (*figure 21 (c)*).

Cunningham Hole. A Cunningham hole (named after Briggs Cunningham of the USA who invented it in the 6-metre days) is a means of putting more tension on a mainsail luff which is already out to its marks and so cannot be pulled farther by its halyard, without breaking the rules, as the sail would stretch beyond the permitted distance. It consists of an eye worked into the luff tabling about 6 to 8 in up from the tack, through which a line is passed so that it can pull down on the hole to add tension to the luff when required, thus drawing the sail's flow farther forward (*figure 58*). Besides more pull on the luff, tension on the Cunningham hole will cause a bunch of wrinkles in the tack area, but these are a small price to pay for the benefits gained. Its main use is in light or medium weather sails, which can then be made right up to size for their normal use (and therefore don't have to be set short of the bands as described above) and where the flow can be drawn forward again by use of the Cunningham hole if the wind increases. Equally, a heavy weather mainsail should always have one, so that the effect of really strong winds pushing the belly right aft can be counteracted by harsh use of the device. It can also sometimes give a new lease of life to an old sail where the flow has been blown aft with the passage of time; it is also useful for removing the leech crease caused by bending the mast. The

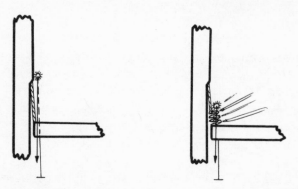

Fig. 58. Cunningham Hole. The object of the Cunningham hole has been fully explained on page 75. It should be rigged so that it can be pulled down quickly and without too much effort. A permanently rove line is essential, preferably with some sort of jamming cleat. Don't let the resulting wrinkles worry you—they are the lesser of two evils when compared with the alternative of a mainsail with a full after belly.

secret of the Cunningham hole is to have a permanently rigged multi-purchase adjusting line operating easily to a jam cleat; it will then be used often.

Foot Outhaul. Most of what is contained in the previous four paragraphs can be said about the clew outhaul and foot of a mainsail, though without quite the same emphasis; in particular the effect of a Cunningham hole is not so marked on the foot of a sail. On the other hand, easing the *clew* to add flow to the sail will make a big difference to performance on a reach and run.

Jib Halyard

We have seen how a jib needs to have a luff wire slightly tighter than the forestay, and how you have to rely on the pull of the main sheet transmitted through the mast to the forestay in order to keep a straight luff when you have slack rigging. If that were all there was to it, we could stop this section now. But the control luff jib has changed all that.

The sail is hoisted until the luff wire is at the right tension, and I shall assume that we are talking about the close-hauled condition: the

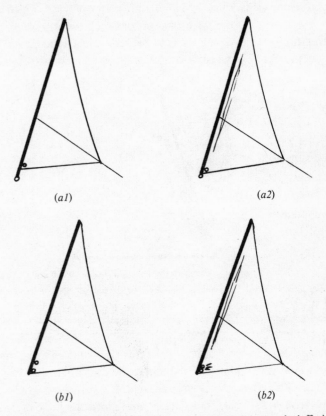

(a1)   *(a2)*

(b1)   *(b2)*

Fig. 59. Control Luff Jib. A control luff jib can be made to slide over the luff wire, so that it stops short of the tack by a few inches when slack (*a1*) and has to be pulled down when further tension is wanted (*a2*). Alternatively, it is made full size and seized to the tack in the usual way, but with little tension on the cloth (*b1*); it then has a Cunningham hole for adjusting tension just like a mainsail (*b2*).

luff wire is accordingly tight. As explained in Chapter 2, the sail itself fits over this luff wire rather like a glove over a finger and it is seized at the head (and sometimes at the tack as well), but the whole of the rest of the luff is loose on the wire and free to float. A line is made fast to an eye in the sail just above the tack, and control of the tension on the luff is exercised in much the same way as a Cunningham hole is used. The basic principles which apply to a mainsail also apply to a jib, but you must remember that there is no tension on the sailcloth at the luff at all from the halyard, which only sets up tension on the wire independently of the sail itself. The control line is thus acting as both halyard and Cunningham hole tensioner as far as induced flow in the cloth is concerned (*figure 59*).

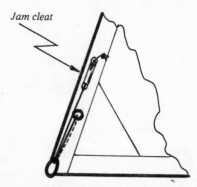

Jam cleat

Fig. 60. *Control Luff Roller Jib.* The system shown in *figure 59* will not work with a jib roller unless special equipment is used, because the control line has to pass down the centre of the drum. Use of a jam cleat sewn to the sail itself is a cheap way of overcoming this problem, although it means that remote control is not possible.

One of the objections to this system is that you can't roll the jib without expensive equipment if you have the control lines leading aft. There are jib rollers on the market on which you can pass the line down through the drum, but if you can't afford the price of one of these there is a cheap way round. Sew one of the smaller jam cleats to the luff of the jib itself, as shown in *figure 60*, and you can have your cake and eat it—control and roll.

Mainsail Twist

As soon as a dinghy comes off the close hauled condition she is said to be on a close reach. This is one of the fastest points of sailing because not only are you pointing exactly where you want to go and the sails are giving more forward and less sideways drive than when beating to windward, but your own speed through the water adds to the speed of the wind to make you go faster. It is, however, important to keep the power developed by the sails pushing you forward as much as possible and sideways as little as possible. Besides trimming the boom and jib sheet to do this (*figures 12* and *13*), you must give some thought to mainsail twist.

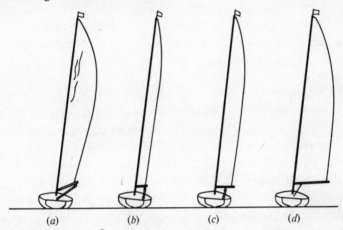

(a) (b) (c) (d)

Fig. 61. Mainsail Twist. If the boom is allowed to rise, the top of the mainsail will twist and be at a finer angle to the wind than the lower half (a). To keep the sail full of wind in the head, therefore, the boom has to be farther in than the foot of the sail would otherwise require.

Use of a full width transom main sheet traveller allows the boom to be freed off to the extent of the traveller, yet still pulled down to stop twist (b). If the traveller is under the centre of the boom instead of on the boat's transom, the boom can be eased further still before it starts to rise (c).

When the sheeting point on the boom is eased beyond the traveller end, the kicking strap takes over the job of holding it down to keep out twist. It has less purchase, so greater tension is required to make it work (d).

First, what is twist? It is the different angle at the head of a sail when compared with that at the foot: the sail actually twists as it nears the top (*figure 61 (a)*). You get the same effect from a jib which is sheeted too far inboard or aft. This means that the top of the sail is at a finer angle to the wind than the rest and will lift first. Or put the other way, to stop the top of the sail lifting, the foot has to be quite a long way inside its best angle and the lower half of the sail thus

79

produces a lot of unnecessary sideways force. If we can reduce twist the lower half of the sail can be eased off and will be pushing forward as much as the upper part, so we shall have a more efficient boat.

Fortunately it is relatively easy to cut down twist: all you have to do is to stop the boom rising as it is freed off. This can be done in two ways. First, a main sheet which travels on a full-width track across the boat will exert a downward pull on the boom until it is a long way out. Secondly, a kicking strap will take over the downward pull when the boom is too far out for the sheet to pull other than inwards (*figures 61 (b), (c),* and *(d)*).

Jib Sheet Lead

You should already have decided the fore and aft position of your jib sheet leads, but it may be that some minor adjustment will be necessary as the result of competition sailing. If the lead is taken forward you will cut down twist, tighten up the leech and add more flow to the foot. A lead farther aft will tighten the foot, free the leech, and increase twist. The former may increase any tendency to backwind shown by the mainsail as, of course, it will if the fairlead is brought more inboard in an attempt to get the boat to point higher.

Sheet Trimming

The effect of the sheet differs from mainsail to jib. A main sheet, apart from its influence on mast bend and twist when close hauled, only allows the sail to free off to leeward when it is further eased and does not let the clew go forward to give the sail more belly. The jib sheet, on the other hand, increases flow by letting the clew forward as it is eased from the hard-in position; it then allows the sail to free off to leeward as it is eased further. Conversely, as the sheet is pulled in the last few inches it flattens the jib both at the luff and the leech—which does not happen in the case of the mainsail. There might be a case here for experimenting with a main sheet attached directly to the clew outhaul in order to give extra flow automatically as the boom is eased off.

Close Hauled: Mainsail. Once the mainsail has been set on the spars to give the shape you want, the main sheet traveller should be used to give the correct boom angle when sailing close hauled. In light airs it should be kept amidships, or even up to windward if this is not going to mean that the leech is trying to pull the boat aft. As the wind increases, so it will get hold of the leech, giving the boat more weather helm and slowing her down; the traveller should be eased to allow the wind to escape more easily and the sheet hardened to cut down twist as much as possible. The degree and timing of adjustments will depend on sea conditions, the basic fullness of the mainsail and more particularly on the crew's ability to keep the boat upright: with a heavy crew and a trapeze or sliding seat, the boom can sometimes be kept amidships with advantage in stronger weather.

Close Hauled: Jib. The jib sheet doesn't have a controllable fairlead like the main sheet (which effectively has this through its traveller) but it does have an effect on the fullness of the sail, as we saw two paragraphs back. In strong winds the sail should be sheeted as hard as possible to prevent this fullness developing and to flatten the leech in particular; in light airs the sheet should be eased to give flow to the sail, which otherwise would not generate enough power.

Reaching: Mainsail. To allow the mainsail to pull as far forward as possible on a reach, the traveller should be eased down to leeward, the lee shroud slackened if levers are fitted, and the sheet freed off to the point just before the luff of the sail starts to lift. It is important to see that maximum power is achieved as forward thrust and minimum as heeling force. The kicking strap should be fairly tight to keep down twist but not so tight that the boom drags along in the water half the time. The harm caused by wind pushing the belly or flow aft into the sail when beating to windward ceases when sailing free, because a full sail with its powerpoint at the mid-way position is the best shape off the wind. If, therefore, you have strapped down your Cunningham hole and gooseneck as hard as they will go (for beating to windward in strong winds) you should ease them both at once—and the clew outhaul too, if possible. You now require a sail with plenty of belly and no hard folds in it. Similarly, unzip the foot, if applicable.

Reaching: Jib. When close hauled, the sheet of a low-cut jib such as a genoa pulls relatively well aft and along the foot. As soon as it is freed on a reach the rearward tension is eased and the clew goes forward, thus giving more flow to the sail. This tends to keep the leech closed, so the fairlead should be moved aft and outboard if possible when the wind comes free, in order to open the slot a bit. If, on the other hand, the jib is tall and narrow with a fairly high-cut

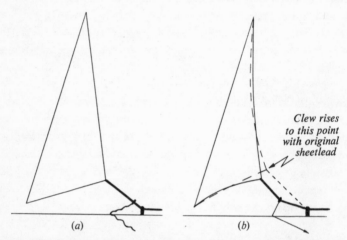

*Clew rises
to this point
with original
sheetlead*

(a)   (b)

Fig. 62. Barber Hauler. A Barber Hauler offers a means of adjusting the jib fairlead to a more forward position. When close hauled, a jib cut low like a genoa usually has more tension along the foot than down the leech. When the sheet is eased on a reach, the clew goes forward and the sail achieves more belly. The reverse is the case with a narrow high-cut sail, however, and the clew tends to rise too much as the sheet is eased and relaxes tension down the leech. The Barber Hauler should then be tightened to lead the sheet down more, and so allow the clew to go forward and give the sail greater fullness on the reach.

foot, the close-hauled lead is usually more down the leech than along the foot. The clew of such a sail rises as soon as the sheet is first eased, when instead we want it to go forward so that more flow is given to the sail. This is particularly true where the clew is some way from the fairlead. To overcome this the brothers Manning and Merritt Barber of California developed the system of adjustment on their International Lightning class boat in 1963' which has been named Barber Hauler after them. This is an eye or thimble free to run along the sheet between the fairlead and jib clew, which can be drawn downwards by a line running through the deck a short distance forward of the fixed fairlead. When the sheet is eased the Barber Hauler is tightened so that the thimble is drawn below the usual line of the sheet and takes over the job of fairlead from the regular fitting. This leads the sheet more downward and allows the clew to ease forward as the sheet is first freed, thus achieving more flow in the sail (*figure 62*). It is, in effect, an adjustable fairlead, so check that your rules allow it before you fit one.

Power Sailing

Power sailing is the art of sailing to windward by freeing the boat just enough to improve speed so that you go upwind faster than the boat which is pointing higher by sailing conventionally close hauled, in the same way that the latter usually goes better than one which is pointing higher still, but pinching. You will fall off to leeward, so sheer speed will decide whether it pays or not (*figure 63*). To make it work, three factors have to be right: sails, angle off the wind, and wind conditions.

Sails. As the name implies, the technique depends on developing more power. To do this sails should be fairly full and, as in the case of those Merlin Rocket dinghies which have been using it with success in England, a large 'free' roach area in the foot of the jib (say, 8 to 10 in) should not be barred by the rules. This roach won't set when beating to windward normally, but will do so if the boat is freed a little and the sheet eased slightly. This freer wind also allows the mainsail clew and tack to be eased and zippers undone. My remarks, a few pages back under Sheet Trimming, about the different effects of main and jib sheets, apply here. It is more belly which is wanted, not a greater sheeting angle, so you do not ease the mainsheet, only the main clew. The extra area in the foot of the jib is also used to advantage and you will gain a significant amount of fullness and power over the close-hauled boat.

Angle. You will soon find by trial and error whether you can make power sailing pay with your boat. If you have to bear away from the

83

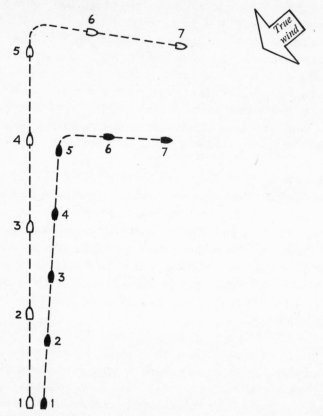

Fig. 63. *Power Sailing.* Power sailing depends on extra speed. If a boat frees off from the close hauled course by about 3° to 4°, full sails with deep roaches will generate more power than those of a boat beating normally to windward. If the balance of angle off and speed is correctly adjusted, the extra speed of the boat power sailing (white boat in this drawing) will more than compensate for the distance gained to windward by the conventional boat (black boat). But, if either speed gain is not enough or the angle off too great, the technique will not pay.

normal close hauled course by more than 3° to 4° to make the sails develop their full power, you will probably lose more ground to leeward than you will be able to make up in speed through the water.

Wind Conditions. The technique only seems to pay in light or in strong conditions. Full sails are needed, anyway, for light winds and smooth water; the extra area gained from the jib foot seems to give the edge on those who are conventionally close hauled, but the amount you free off is critical and needs careful watching if it is to pay. In strong winds the water is often choppy, when it pays to ramp the boat off a bit and push her through it; fuller sails will help this. If, in addition, marginal planing conditions exist and the extra power makes just the difference in getting up on the step, then the advantages are obvious. There seems to be a gap between light and strong conditions where no profit can be derived, and how wide this gap is will depend on your own boat, sails, and technique. In the stronger winds the boat is of course harder to keep upright because not only are you developing more forward thrust but also a lot more heeling force. With a bendy mast and a good heavy crew, however, you can control these heeling forces and take full advantage of the extra power generated to get greater speed—even more so if the crew has a trapeze or a sliding seat.

Trim Tips

Assuming that other factors such as sail shape, boat tuning, and technique are all satisfactory, the following suggestions are offered as ways of altering the speed of a dinghy through use of sails alone.

Note that I say *altering* the speed of a dinghy, not *increasing* it: if you have a particular aspect of sail trim correctly set already, then any alteration can but decrease your speed. We have all, however, raced neck and neck alongside a rival without gaining or losing an inch, and longed for another yard or two of speed (and that's all you need over a couple of hundred yards). The ideas in this section are not necessarily in any particular order, although I suggest that the first ones are more likely to have the desired effect than the later ones. Please don't go blaming me if they lose you a coveted cup—you should try them in practice first, or in less important races, and not wait for the grand occasion before experimenting. Above all, don't be prejudiced by knowing that what you have always done is right—conditions may be different today.

First of all bear in mind the general principles of sail shape:

Wide sheeting base	Full mainsail
	Strong winds
	Reaching conditions
	More speed, less point
Narrow sheeting base	High point, less speed
	Backwinding
	Flat mainsail
	Light winds

Jib Halyard. This is often too slack, especially with tight rigging and wire luff sails. Get another inch or two up on it.

Jib Sheet. A boat is generally more sensitive to the jib sheet than to the main sheet. Try easing the jib an inch or two on the beat, particularly in the lighter winds.

Jib Fairlead. This affects the curve of the jib in both planes and thus has a marked bearing on perfoormance. Movement outboard will give more speed and less backwinding but will stop you pointing so high; movement inboard has the opposite effect. There is some merit in a narrow jib angle on faster boats (of the scow type, for example) to help you point really high. This is directly contrary to the concept of power sailing and you will have to decide for yourself which technique suits your boat best. Putting the fairlead forward gives more flow to the jib and tightens the leech (more speed and less point, with a greater risk of backwinding the mainsail), while movement backwards will flatten the foot and slack off the leech with opposite effect.

Mainsail Clew. Easing the clew will give the mainsail more flow low down where it does most good and where any attendant increase in heeling force will do least harm. This is worth a try, even in the stronger wind ranges, particularly if you have a wide mainsheet traveller.

Mainsheet Traveller. You may be easing it off too soon or too late (probably the former): change the rhythm.

86

Spinnaker Sheet. If it is too tight it will kill the boat. Ease it all you can (but watch out for rhythmic rolling downwind; harden the sheet a little to prevent oscillation).

Spinnaker Pole Angle. Try changing the pole angle: an inch aft first, then an inch forward if that doesn't work.

Spinnaker Pole Height. Move it up or down a few inches and watch for results. If necessary, on a reach, try it hard down on the stem head to straighten the luff of the spinnaker, or poked well up into the sky to disengage the luff from the jib if both are being carried at once.

Spinnaker Halyard. Try easing the halyard about 6 in when on a reach. This will disengage the head of the spinnaker from the disturbed airflow near the mast.

6 Spinnakers

Spinnaker Cloth

Not until nylon was developed did spinnakers enjoy a change of material from the light cotton which was used for so long. Dacron and Terylene made everyone think twice in the 1950s, but spinnakers need a certain amount of stretch if they are to take up their shape, and nylon is better for this. It has been shown repeatedly that spinnaker cloth should not allow air to pass through the material or loss of thrust will result as the pressure equalises on each side of the sail. When this is added to the other requirements for a good spinnaker cloth, nylon seems to be the best answer at present, mainly falling short in its rot-proof qualities. Spinnaker requirements include:

Porosity. I have already mentioned the importance of low porosity.

Lightness. A cloth of 25 to 75 gm/m^2 is needed so that the sail hasn't too much weight to lift and fill in the relatively low wind speeds which often exist when the boat is running away from the wind, thus cutting down apparent wind speed.

Strength. When a boat is not running but sailing across or into the wind and thereby increasing its force, the large area of a spinnaker means that it has a good deal of weight in it. For those who may be interested, pressure in a sail under given wind conditions can be roughly calculated by using a formula which reads $W = 0.004V^2A$, where W is the total weight of wind in the sail in lb, V is the relative wind speed in mph, and A is the sail area in sq ft. Thus a spinnaker of

225 ft^2 in a 25 mph relative reaching wind (which need be no more than 15 mph true) will have over a quarter of a ton in it.

Power to Repel Water. It is useful if the spinnaker will not absorb a lot of water and will dry quickly when it is wet.

Rot Proof. The cloth should not be too badly affected by heat, cold, dryness, industrial smoke, sunlight, or water.

Low Stretch. A certain amount of stretch is useful to help the sail develop its shape in the wind, but not so much that it distorts.

A porous cloth can have its airtightness improved by the addition of fillers in the finishing stage in the same way as Terylene or Dacron. But, also in the same way, the chemicals will eventually break down to leave the original slack weave. This will allow air to pass through and the sail will lose drive.

Tests. You can test spinnaker cloth by crumpling it in your hand and looking for crazing of the fillers in much the same way as for other sailcloth. You can also learn a good deal about its porosity by trying to breathe through it. A little experience will soon tell you which is a good tight weave and which is loose. Try the 'breathalyser' test both before and after crumpling the sample; you may be surprised at the difference.

One final point to remember about nylon: it obeys the same laws of physical behaviour as Dacron and Terylene. Moreover, because we are dealing with a light material the effects are greater, particularly as regards bias stretch and sunlight deterioration.

Outline Design

As with mainsails and jibs, outline design of a spinnaker is the job of the naval architect, who decides the basic size to make the sail. This in turn is sometimes dictated by an already existing rule, but when dealing with a new class of dinghy it is more usually a matter for the designer's personal decision made in the light of his expert knowledge and experience, much as the lines of the boat are the fruit of his

89

training and skill. There is nothing you or I can do to alter a particular sailplan even if we wanted to, so we need not concern ourselves here with how it was reached.

Flow Design

In considering flow design (the amount and position of belly) of a spinnaker we have to consider what happens to the wind in the sail. On a reach the airflow behaves very much as in a jib in that it blows from luff to leech; on a dead run it flows from the centre towards both sides, with a bleed downwards at the foot.

Figure 64 shows how a spinnaker with a deep 'nose' is not only

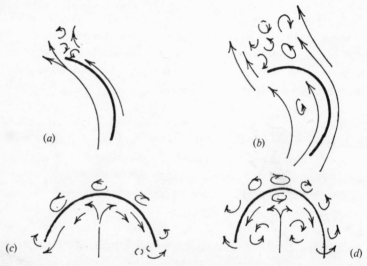

Fig. 64. Flat- and Full-cut Spinnakers. (*a*) and (*b*) in this drawing show a flat- and a full-cut spinnaker on a reach. The flat sail shows a fair airflow across the sail, starting with a clean entry. The full sail would probably never set at all because of the angle at which the wind strikes the luff. Even if it did stand all right, the airflow would be turbulent because of the sharp changes in direction it has to make; in addition, the leech returns to windward and offers the same disadvantages as a curling leech on a jib.

(*c*) and (*d*) show the same effect on a run. (*c*) allows air to reach the surface of the sail and then divide each way, thus spreading the sail and presenting the maximum area to the wind. (*d*) has a pocket of dead air in the depth of its centre, and the turbulence this brings only serves to disturb the free flow of air towards the leeches; the sail will therefore be narrower in the head than (*c*).

90

more inefficient on a reach but also loses out on a run to a sail which is cut flatter in the head, because dead air collects in the deep part of the sail and disturbs the airflow.

The sailmaker must keep stretch in the sail within set limits. To do this he tries to arrange the cloth panels in the sail so that stress lines run along the threadlines of the cloth and not on the bias. But directions of stress in a spinnaker are many and varied, and this sometimes results in sails which have more cloths in them than a patchwork quilt. Different cuts and patterns have their day as a new vogue appears, but the horizontally cut sail—either with or without a centre seam—takes a good deal of beating for all round use as it offers advantages in control of bias stretch where it is most important (at the leeches and in the head) coupled with a certain simplicity of manufacture.

Airflow

The thing to remember about spinnakers is that for most of their active careers they have the wind blowing *across* them from luff to leech, just like a jib. They do not, however, have the advantage of a jib's straight luff and flat leech. Nevertheless, the same basic principles apply, including slot effect, backwinding, and a need for maximum forward thrust and minimum heeling force.

Only when the wind is within about 10° either side of dead aft is the object of a spinnaker to present the greatest area of sail to the wind so that most drag is achieved and the boat blown downwind. Even here there are other factors such as getting the sail into undisturbed wind, ensuring that the thrust is forward and not angled off to one side, and seeing that the spinnaker sits symmetrically with clew and tack evenly balanced.

The spinnaker can thus be likened to an extra large jib which has the advantage (for the initiated) or the disadvantage (for the not so fortunate) of an adjustable tack as well as an adjustable clew. Its setting and trim would take up a book on their own, so I propose to limit my remarks here to some points of theory followed by a few general observations.

The way in which the wind travels across both spinnaker and jib on a reach is shown in *figure 65 (a)* and (*b*). Subject to certain

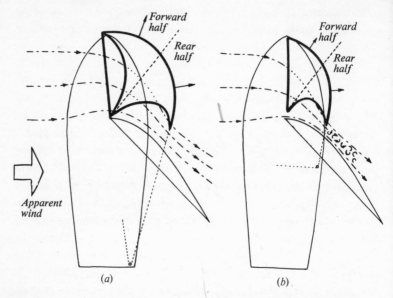

Fig. 65. Comparison of Spinnaker and Jib on a Reach. A spinnaker has greater area than a jib, so it pays to reach with it if that area can be made to do useful work. Remember that, if a spinnaker has more area pulling forwards, it often has the same superiority pulling sideways as well. It is a good idea to divide the spinnaker mentally down the middle, and ask yourself what the rear half is doing. If it is pulling aft, you need to consider very carefully whether this is causing so much heel and brake effect that it is cancelling out the forward pull. The rear half of a jib seldom pulls aft at all (unless it has been blown out of shape, so that the flow is nearer the leech than the luff), therefore that part of the sail only adds to heel effect without actually braking the boat; this ensures that the efforts of the front half of a jib are not cancelled out as they can be in a spinnaker close reaching.

This explains why it is important at all times, and particularly on a reach, to keep as much spinnaker pulling forwards as possible: you are, in effect, keeping as little of it pulling sideways and backwards as possible. Whether a spinnaker or a jib is better on a particular reach, therefore, depends not only on the relative sizes of the two sails and the closeness of the reach, but also on how the spinnaker can be set and sheeted on the boat to reduce pull rearward.

considerations, therefore, the larger sail will exert the greater total force for any given wind and boat speed. The spinnaker's main advantage over a jib is thus one of size.

But you should remember that not only will a spinnaker give more forward thrust than a jib, it will also give more heeling force. The time comes on a close reach when the larger sail may fill and draw, but it is so closely strapped alongside that a decent-sized jib would be more efficient. This moment depends not only on the wind conditions and how flat the spinnaker is, but also mainly on how much bigger it is than the jib which would be put on instead.

In light and medium winds, of course, both spinnaker and jib can often be used together if the one does not interfere with the free air of the other. This depends largely on the angle of the relative wind (they usually set happily together with the wind within an arc 15° either side of the beam) and also on the way the sails are cut, and trimmed to avoid taking each other's wind. But in reaching conditions where the two sails are not used together a rule of thumb can be stated that a properly cut dinghy spinnaker will pay with the apparent wind 5° forward of the beam for each amount by which the spinnaker is larger than the jib which would otherwise be used. Thus if the spinnaker is five times bigger than the jib (as large a difference as is normally met in dinghies) the larger sail will have the advantage with the apparent wind 25° forward of the beam. The more usual area ratio of three or four to one brings the angle down to 15° to 20°: anything less and the jib is big enough to drive her better. Don't forget that this is a generalisation for use in winds around force 3 to 4; whether it over- or understates the situation will vary not only with wind strength and class but also from helmsman to helmsman as things get down to the final crunch: skill.

To Spi or not to Spi

One of the first decisions, therefore, is often whether to set a spinnaker at all. I am not concerned here with tactics nor with psychological warfare, but even if it is agreed that the wind is in the right direction, you may think that it is blowing too hard. The boat is pretty near her maximum speed anyway, so why bother with the thing? The point to realise here is that there are moments in even the strongest blow when a boat under main and jib alone would fall below top speed. It is for these infrequent lulls that you must hoist the kite if you want to keep motoring flat out all the time. Other things being favourable, therefore, it usually pays to use a spinnaker if control of the boat can be maintained.

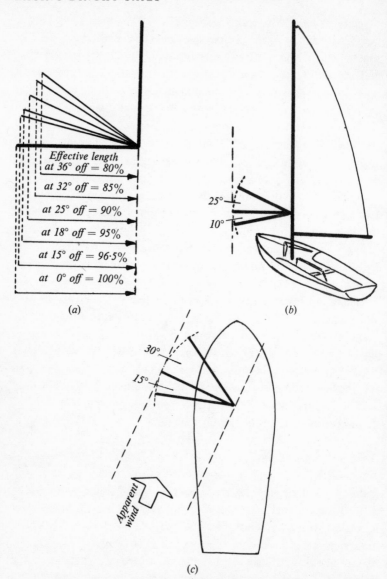

Fig. 66. *Effective Spinnaker Pole Length according to Angle.* The outer end of the spinnaker pole, with the tack of the sail attached to it, is farthest from the nearest point on the mast (and thus from the disturbing influence of the mainsail) when the pole is at right-angles to the mast. This distance will reduce as the pole is allowed to stray from 90° and, for the mathematically inclined, it varies with the cosine of the

Once you have decided to use the sail you should lose no time in hoisting it. You can sometimes gain several places by slick spinnaker work on rounding the weather mark in close company with other boats who are slow to break out their 'chutes. Equally, you should hang on to it until the last moment, relying on well-practised drill to get it down and away only seconds before the leeward mark.

Pole Angle

As one of the objects is to keep the spinnaker away from the disturbed airflow round the mainsail, the tack should be as far away from the mast in both the horizontal and vertical planes as possible. This means that the spinnaker pole should be at right angles to both the mast and the wind (*figures 66 (a)*, *(b)*, and *(c)*).

There are exceptions to this rather bald rule, but you won't go far wrong if you stick pretty close to it. In light winds the pole can be about 10° to 15° farther aft to stop the head of the sail falling away too much. In heavy weather you should let it go forward a bit and trim the sheet harder in order to reduce any tendency to roll and to aid in control: it may not always be possible in gusty conditions to trim the sheet quickly enough to stop the sail collapsing, so a little in hand will help. You will see from *figure 66 (c)* that you won't lose much offset if the pole is up to 15° off the right angle.

Pole Height

Dinghies don't always have means of altering the height of their spinnaker poles at the mast end. The following remarks, therefore, may have to be read with the idea in mind that it is only the outer end of the pole which can be altered. Another glance at *figure 66 (a)* will show that the pole has to be more than 20° off the right angle in the

---

angle by which it strays. You can see the precise effect from *(a)*: the loss is only 5 per cent of length at 18° off, but the amount then goes up rapidly, so that 20 per cent is lost with the pole only twice as far from its proper line.

I have drawn the pole both horizontally *(b)* and vertically *(c)* with typical angles to show the effect, because the same principles apply when looking down on the boat. The aim here is to get the sail spread across the wind as much as possible, and the pole should be at or near right angles to the apparent wind to achieve this maximum coverage.

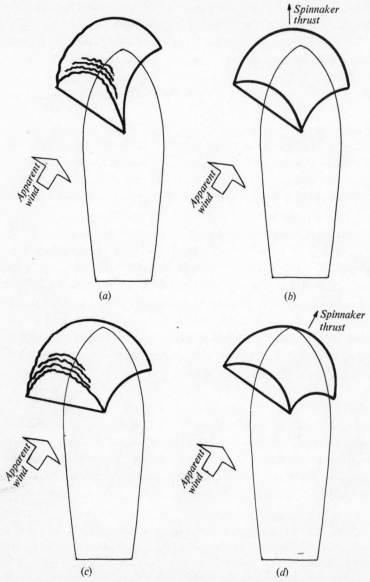

Fig. 67. Spinnaker Sheet Adjustment. The object of spinnaker sheet adjustment is to get the sail pulling forwards and not sideways, as we have already seen in figure 65. If the sheet is eased too much, as in (a), the luff will fall in and the whole sail will collapse if it is not corrected. Proper trim on a broad reach should enable the whole

vertical or the fore and aft planes before more than a 5 per cent reduction in its effective length takes place.

The basic aim in deciding pole height is to see that the tack and clew of the spinnaker are the same height above the water; this will ensure that the sail, being symmetrical, is not twisted into a poor aerodynamic shape. The outer end of the pole should be positioned so that the tack will be level with the clew, and then the pole is squared to the apparent wind. When the sheet has been trimmed so that the sail is on the point of falling in at the luff, the height of the clew and tack should be compared and any further minor adjustment made. If the tack is higher than the clew the leech will tend to fall inwards, close the slot and backwind the mainsail.

In light weather the pole should be moderately low to straighten the luff and reduce the amount of sail which has to be lifted before it fills; it may then slowly be raised as the sail fills and the free clew lifts. In these circumstances aerodynamic shape of the sail takes second place to getting it to fill at all. As the wind increases to force 2 so the pole can be raised to normal height. In medium winds and stronger it sometimes pays when reaching with both spinnaker and jib to raise the pole above the usual angle until it is at right angles to the jib luff. This gets the sail a little farther away from the luff of the jib, thus helping to get it into undisturbed air.

Sheet

Once the pole has been settled, the spinnaker is in basic trim and further adjustments must be made on the sheet.

The sail should be evenly balanced so that tack and clew are both about the same height and also the same distance aft of the bow. Bearing in mind that every bit that the sail can be angled to give forward thrust cuts down the damaging heeling force, the sheet must

---

sail to pull forward efficiently as in (b) but if, with the sheet trimmed correctly, the pole is then squared too far aft, the sail will collapse again as in (c).

The most common fault in spinnaker sheet trim is to sheet the sail too hard as in (d); even though the pole is correctly square to the wind, the drive of the sail is partly sideways so loss of speed must result. You can often tell this is happening because the foot of the spinnaker starts to bear on the forestay; if you can't ease the sheet and keep the sail full, the pole is probably too far aft and must also go forward.

usually be eased as much as possible. In practice, the first sign that the sheet is being eased off too much is that the luff of the sail collapses as the wind gets behind it; the object ideally is to keep the luff on the quiver and you are then sure that as much of the sail as possible is pulling forward in driving force. *Figure 67* helps show the reasoning behind this, and proper application to the task requires the sheet to be repeatedly eased and hardened as the crew feels for the first tremble of the luff and then stops full collapse taking place by hardening in again. This close control is by no means always possible in gusty conditions, so a more settled trim then has to be adopted which will be closer sheeted than the optimum in order to avoid unexpected and sudden collapse of the sail. It should be checked for any possible freeing of the wind from time to time.

It is in light to medium weather that correct spinnaker trim pays the greatest dividends. When the wind is really blowing, your boat soon reaches her maximum hull speed, so the finer points are wasted.

7 Care and Maintenance

Lowering Sail
Always pull sails down by the luff. Dragging at the unsupported leech will cause localised stretching and give rise to fluttering and creases.

Hosing Down
Sails should be hosed down after use where salt water or dirt have got on them. While these will not harm synthetic cloth chemically,

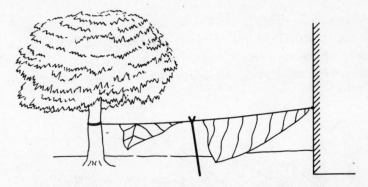

Fig. 68. Hanging Sails to Dry. Sails should be hung to dry so that their weight is supported by the luff, which has reinforcement in the shape of a wire, rope, or tape. If the leech is called upon to do the task, it will stretch out of shape.

salt crystals or particles of dirt will work into the weave and saw away at the fibres causing the finish of the cloth to break down, particularly if it has been reinforced with chemical fillers.

After hosing, sails should be hung by the head and tack to dry. In this way weight is not thrown on the leech, which would cause it to stretch (*figure 68*).

Bagging Sails

Most of you know that synthetic sails should be kept in big bags to avoid the creases which would be caused by crushing into small ones. What many forget, however, is that this crushing can still take place after the sails have been bagged. It's no good having sails gently put into roomy bags if you go and throw the rudder or a couple of boat chocks on them as they sit in the corner.

Even if you are careful about their bags, sails will eventually crease in the wrong places if they are not folded before they are put away. All creases in sails are wrong, but it is not possible to avoid them completely. What can be done is to see that haphazard creasing does not take place near the leech, or you can be quite certain that bad permanent creases will settle in the leech tabling—the worst place to have them. This will immediately give rise to 'motorboating', which is doubtless familiar to you and which is so bad for the helmsman's morale due to its unsettling effect.

Folding a Mainsail. Figure 69 shows two ways of folding a mainsail. It can be argued that the one which gives horizontal creases is the better of the two, because the creases offer less interference to a smooth flow of air across the surface. But I prefer to ring the changes

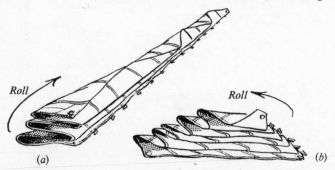

Roll (a) *Roll* (b)

Fig. 69. Folding a Mainsail. Avoid creasing the leech of the sail when folding it, and don't go and fold it carefully only to stow heavy gear on top of the sailbag afterwards. It is a good idea to roll the sail round the boom if you are putting it away for any length of time.

100

so that creases do not get the chance to settle in one spot. Fastidious owners with plenty of room at home only fold their sails for the journey between home and clubhouse; you should certainly take them from their bags and flake them out (in the guest-room, perhaps?) if you are not going to use them for several weeks. If the sail has a zipper, leave it unzipped when folding the sail or you risk the teeth disengaging for a short length where it may be bent in a fold.

Folding a Jib. Figure 70 shows how to fold a jib. Note that the window is carefully placed on the outside of the last roll, so that it does not have to be bent round too sharp a corner. The sailbag should protect the window from scratches.

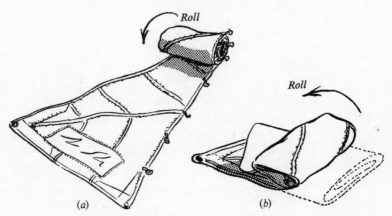

Fig. 70. Folding a Jib. Roll the sail down its luff wire from head to tack, thus making a tube stretching towards the clew. This is then stowed in its turn by rolling from tack to clew. Be careful not to bend any window.

Folding a Spinnaker. Spinnaker nylon is so thin that creases quickly blow out. It is therefore not important from this point of view to fold your spinnaker. If you have a patent way of setting it from its bag, you may care to see that it is put away all ready for hoisting. A good crew, however, will probably undo it all again at the start of the next day's sailing, to satisfy himself that it has been done properly. So it is probably best not to bother in the first place, it being more important

101

to see that the spinnaker is free from tears and is completely dry, not only from the mildew point of view but so that it will be nice and light for possible ghosting conditions next time out.

Cleaning Sails

Besides the regular hosing down with fresh water which most dinghy sailors give their sails, cleaning off the more stubborn stains will make a suit last longer. A guide to the problem is given in ICI Fibres' pamphlet *Laundering and Dry Cleaning of Terylene*, which they kindly allowed me to publish in full in *Sails*. The following are my suggestions for simplified treatment of some of the more usual problems and are given in all good faith, but no responsibility is accepted nor warranty given or implied.

Warning. Normal care in the use of chemicals should be observed, especially as far as fumes, poisoning, burns, and fire are concerned: ensure plenty of fresh air while working; do not smoke (not only because of the fire hazard but also because some chemical cleaners produce poisonous fumes when their vapour is drawn through a burning cigarette); wash any neat chemicals off your body or clothes immediately; avoid naked flames or a lot of heat. Although many of the treatments given here are free from harmful chemicals, some are not, and it is a good idea to get into the habit of always taking these precautions. In addition, you should only use containers made of stainless steel, porcelain, enamel, or polythene, and not galvanised iron or alloy; keep strong chemicals away from galvanised luff wires, thimbles, slides, etc. Finally, always rinse out after cleaning so as to remove the danger of a 'high water mark'.

Washing

Synthetic dinghy sails can usually be washed in the bath. Don't be afraid to use a scrubbing brush (a sailmaker will probably have an industrial rotary scrubber) and use water as hot as your hand can bear, with bar soap (Lifebuoy is as good as any) or any proprietary liquid detergent such as Stergene, Quix, or a similar brand. If this won't shift local areas of general dirt, soak the affected part in neat detergent overnight before washing.

102

Stains

The following suggestions refer only to white Terylene or Dacron sails. Stains on coloured sails should be treated only after specialist advice.

Adhesive Numbers. Many adhesives used with stick-on racing numbers can be dissolved by soaking in benzene; any adhesive remaining on the sail after the numbers have been removed may be rubbed away with a benzene soaked rag. In the absence of benzene, try one of the biological soap powders.

Blood. Biological cleaners are best for removing blood and other protein stains, but there is a danger that those of them which contain optical brighteners may have an adverse effect on dyestuffs, some special resins, and also on the bolt rope; this is particularly true where the sail is left to soak for longer periods (overnight) for the enzymes to 'digest' the protein. Biotex and Big S contain no optical brighteners and should be suitable; treat stubborn stains by soaking for an hour before washing out. Keep adhesive numbers out of the solution or they may come off.

Mildew. Scrub lightly with a stiff dry brush to remove as much of the mould as possible, then soak for two or three hours in a mixture containing a domestic bleach; one part Domestos to ten parts of water will do a fair job. Wash well afterwards and repeat if necessary, but be prepared for only partial success because mildew stains are hard to get rid of.

Oil, Grease, or Wax. These stains may be tackled with a proprietary grease remover such as Polyclens, Thawpit, Dabitoff, or Genklene. For heavy stains, mix one part of liquid detergent with two parts of Polyclens or similar cleaner and brush well into the fabric. Leave for 15 minutes and then wash off with warm water. These treatments will not remove stains caused by the fine metallic particles which are often associated with lubricants. Such stains have to be tackled with special acid solutions outside the scope of a day-to-day book of this nature (see *Sails* for fuller instructions).

103

Paint. All paint is difficult to remove unless treated without delay with turpentine, turpentine substitute, or something similar. Avoid using paint strippers based on alkalis (and most of them are); solvents such as chloroform, however, may be successful on dried paint.

Pitch and Tar. While these have their own more sophisticated cures beyond the scope of this book, you will find that they respond as well as anything to the same treatment as for oil, grease, and wax stains. Complete cleaning will always be difficult.

Varnish. Polyurethane varnish is hard to remove once it has dried, but you could try chloroform; shellac varnish can be removed with methylated spirits or alcohol. Any varnish which is still wet should respond to turpentine.

Ironing Sails

The best advice about ironing sails is *Don't*. But there are those who do it, and who do it successfully, so I must obviously say some more. Be careful of isolated patches of the sail becoming overheated. This will cause localised melting of the filaments, which will fuse together and distort the cloth and which can never be cured. In addition, a heat of 70° C (160° F) causes shrinkage, so you must be careful even if you are satisfied that you will not actually melt the filaments. Use a heat-controlled iron on the coolest setting and switch it off before starting; do not leave it in contact with one part of the sail for more than one or two seconds.

Reproofing Sails

The chemicals which are put into some synthetic sailcloths will eventually work their way out of the weave, and the sail will be the worse for it. As these fillers have been forced into the material straight from the loom, under pressure between heated rollers, they cannot be put back again once the cloth has been cut and sewn into a sail. There is nothing, therefore, which anyone—professional or amateur—can do to restore resin filling permanently and successfully to a synthetic sail.

Laying Up
When putting away your sails for the winter, besides thoroughly washing and cleaning them, have a good inspection for repairs. A stitch at laying-up time will certainly save nine a week after you start sailing again.

Ancillary Items. Check over all *eyes* and *cringles*. The one most likely to give trouble is the jib tack, which supports the full weight of the jib and mast and may be twisted if you have a jib furling gear; it also spends quite a bit of its time under water. In wire eyes, and eyelets worked or punched into the sailcloth, there is usually a metal *thimble* or *turnover* inserted to protect the wire or seizing from the chafing effects of shackles and pins; this protecting piece may distort and start to pull out of the eye. If caught early enough it can often be hammered back again; otherwise it may need replacing by a new one put in with a punch and die. *Piston* or *snap hanks* should be looked at, and a drop or two of oil put on the plunger (not more, if you don't want it to get all over your sails); check their lashings. *Nylon twist hanks* chafe readily on the luff wire and they should be examined carefully. *Wire jib clips* can get bent and weakened. *Zippers* on sails are usually made from nylon so they need little attention save a check to see that the stitching is still good and all the teeth are there. The *slider* itself will probably be metal, however, so it should be checked for corrosion and given a spot of oil or light grease. *Lashings* for clew outhaul or tack fitting should have suspect whippings renewed, as should the ends of *sheets*, which should also be checked for chafe on blocks and jam cleats. *Battens* need attention to see that they don't have jagged edges or splits in the ends; a lick of varnish won't hurt wooden battens, and you can reinforce thin ends by binding with adhesive tape. Look at the *headboard* to see that it is not split or coming away from the sail, and check any *window* for splits or scratches. Finally, see that the *sailbag* itself is in good shape, for it has to protect the sail from dirt and damage for most of its life.

Chafe. Stitching sits on the surface of Terylene instead of bedding in, and likely points of chafe are jib leeches, where they rub on shrouds, spreaders and odd projections on the mast, and mainsail luffs, where

105

they chafe on the shrouds when running; batten pockets can go at both ends, particularly where they rub on shrouds when running. Look carefully at the head of your spinnaker where the swivel is attached, thus giving it play to work from side to side and attack the stitching; the foot of the spinnaker may well chafe on the forestay under certain wind conditions. It goes without saying that you should always try to remove the cause of any recurrent chafing if possible.

Ropes. If the bolt rope is sewn outside the sail along its entire length, check it for security, particularly at the head and clew. If the rope is sleeved into the tabling or tape, check that the seizings at each end are firmly attached and that it has not picked up splinters from wooden spars. A conventional tabling, being made from sailcloth panels with seams where these join, is more likely to pick up splinters than a luff tape; it will also tend to chafe where the rather thick seams rub on the groove. If the luff has a tape (usually with a rope as well), check that the machine stitching is unbroken and that it is firmly attached at head and clew.

Wires. Have a close look at all luff wires. Galvanised wire will rust away unless it has been well protected; stainless steel does not always live up to its name and may cause discolouration of synthetic cloth (which does not necessarily harm the material, but is unsightly and hard to remove). You should pay special attention to the tack, where the protective coating has been disturbed during the splicing or swaging process, and where the wire gets wettest. Jib luff wires are usually hidden inside the tabling so it is difficult to see any damage; bend the wire back and forth, and listen carefully for any cracking or chafing noises which would betray a partly stranded wire, especially in the bottom foot or so of the sail. If your spinnaker has wires in the luff/leeches, check them for the same faults and also measure one against the other for equal length: if one is longer than the other, it is probably broken. If any wire is suspect, its replacement is best done by a sailmaker.

Storing Sails

When synthetic sails are put away for any length of time they should ideally be loosely flaked in a dry storage room; a weatherproof attic is as good as anywhere, provided the sails are not forgotten. They should be turned over once or twice during the winter and checked to see that the attic is indeed dry (don't forget that mildew can form on wet synthetics where dirt is also present) and that rats and mice haven't chewed off bits of them for nest-making purposes.

Where a good airy space is not available for spreading out, the sails may be hung up. Roll the mainsail round its boom to avoid creases and hang it over the rafters in the garage. The jib can hang down against the wall alongside, supported by the head and tack and with the clew hanging free; this keeps the weight off the leech.

The third best alternative is to leave them folded and stow them away in a dry cupboard. Wives please note that I do not actually specify 'in the linen cupboard', although this obviously fits the requirement admirably ...

Fitting Out

If you did all that you should have done at the end of the season, you should have few problems when it comes to fitting out. If you did not make a good job of laying up, get out your sails as soon as you can and go through the items listed above. In any event, put a second drop of oil on all hanks, snap hooks, and shackles, and check zippers for ease of operation. Make sure that spar grooves are smooth-running (a light coating of paraffin wax will help here) and that all wire is free from barbed strands, and you are then ready to go.

If you find any repairs which need the attention of your sailmaker, get the sail away as soon as possible, but don't hope for too fast a service if you have left it late.

8 Repairs

Benchwork

It's no good making a bald recommendation to repair a sail unless I first give some idea of how it is to be done. I cannot, of course, tell you how to become a sailmaker in the course of three (or even four) easy lessons—and I can't even assure you that you will be much better off from the rather fuller detail which appears in *Sails*. I can, however, tell you about some of the simpler stitches, and the thread and needles to use, and then leave you to get plenty of practice.

Sewing Machine. A domestic sewing machine may certainly be used for sail repairs. It is best if the machine can sew a cross-stitch, or zig-zag as it is also called. This allows the canvas to work slightly when sailing without putting too great a strain on the stitching. Make sure that the tension is adjusted so that the stitches link together inside the cloth rather than above or below, where they can be broken by chafe.

Thread. Synthetic thread is best for use with synthetic cloth, both for machine and hand sewing; most sailmakers will sell you a spool or two (and will give further advice on which ones to buy). Hand sewing thread (or seaming twine) is measured in England by its breaking strain in pounds, and runs from 1 to 8, or thereabouts. A rough guide to the correct hand thread for a particular cloth is that breaking strain in pounds of the thread is half the cloth weight in ounces per square yard; thus a cloth of 4 or 5 oz will need a 2 lb thread. You can use machine thread for hand work on spinnakers. If you are roping, working an eye, or sewing a particularly thick or heavy part

108

of the sail (say, a heavy weather mainsail clew) you should ideally go up a pound or two in thread weight, but you will not want to have too many different threads in your ditty box, so use two parts of the 2-lb thread instead of the more usual one.

Needles. Sailmakers' needles are sized according to the British wire gauge. This ensures continuation of the illogical reasoning which bedevils all sailmaking, such as making a hole with a number 13 cutter for a number 2 eyelet to be clenched with a number 4 punch; or sewing a 5 oz cloth with a 2 lb thread using a number 18 needle. It is all part of the conspiracy to shroud the sailmaker's craft in mumbo jumbo so that the layman shall not learn too much, too quickly. You should get enough practice so that you do not have to use a needle which is too big for the task just because you are not able to control the smaller, correct, size. Too large a needle will make large holes with the danger of wrinkles; too small a needle will result in uneven workmanship and worse wrinkles. You should get by on dinghy sails with sizes 17 and 18, plus a domestic needle for use on your spinnaker. Dull the point of one of your 17s and keep it for roping; it will then more easily pass between the lay of the rope without picking up part of a strand. If you find a 17 too small, don't go larger than a 16 whatever else you do, for a 15 would be much too big and clumsy for dinghy work.

Sailmaker's Sewing Palm. A sewing palm is not difficult to get used to, particularly for the rough work which you will start on. You will probably be a bit clumsy at first, so get a bit of practice on some spare cloth before you have to use it for real repairs. Make sure you don't buy a roping palm which, having a deeper set needle guard to take the longer needle used for roping (it is a size or two larger), will make it hard to hold the shorter sewing needles when they are back against the guard. You can usually tell a roping palm by its built-up thumb protection.

All Stitching. For dinghy sails, thread should be single part (i.e. not doubled) instead of the more usual two part for hand-sewing larger sails; it will still be thicker than the machine thread you will be repairing. The exception to this, as I said above, is where you are roping, working an eye, or sewing a thick part of the sail, where the doubled strand will make a stronger job of it and save using a heavier thread; you may even work a specially large eye using four parts on occasions. If it is not ready-waxed, draw the thread three or four times across a beeswax block to stop it unravelling while sewing, and to make it last better afterwards; a candle will do at a pinch if you have no beeswax. No true sailmaker will ever knot the thread as a stopper when starting a seam, but it is the easiest way to prevent the first stitch pulling out and you need not be too proud to do it (who is

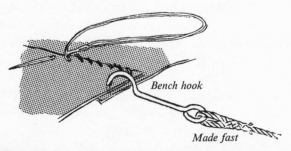

Fig. 71. The Bench Hook. A bench hook goes into one end of the work and is tied by a line away to one side. One hand then tensions the cloth against the pull of the bench hook, while the other does the sewing; the result is much steadier work. This drawing also shows the principle of the flat seaming, or tabling, stitch.

ever going to look, anyway?). A bench hook (*figure 71*) stuck into the cloth and tied away to one side will keep tension on the work and make sewing easier and neater.

Round Stitch. If the edge of the sail has to be re-sewn, for instance the outer end of a batten pocket, spread the work across your knees, start at the left and push the needle up and away from you, using the palm to push the eye of the needle and transferring to the finger and thumb as the needle passes from side to side of the cloth; this is done in a smooth movement which comes with practice, and you can get the general idea from *figure 72*. Pull the thread tight with your left hand, bring the needle back towards you across the top of the work and down again ready for the next stitch.

110

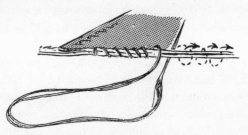

Fig. 72. Round Stitch. This drawing shows how the round stitch is done; it is used when the very edge of a sail has to be sewn.

Tabling Stitch. Where a seam or patch has to be sewn in the middle of the sail it will not be possible to push the needle through the work from one side to the other without having to turn the whole sail over in an unwieldy process to push it back again. This means that it must be pushed down through and back up again all in one movement. This is known as the Flat Seaming Stitch and is shown in *figure 71*. It is best to work from right to left, with the bench hook tied away to the right, pushing the needle towards your left shoulder as it enters the canvas. It is a useful dodge to spread a piece of thick canvas over your knees before you start, as you will then be better able to hear or feel the point of the needle if it just 'skins' or pricks into this protection before coming up through the work again, thus saving you from sewing your own clothing in with the sail.

Sailmaker's Darn. This stitch is useful for gathering the two sides of a tear, either temporarily or as a permanent repair, and it is the same as the domestic herringbone stitch. Stitching is from left to right, and

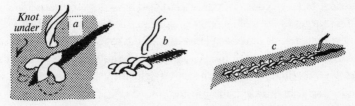

Fig. 73. A Sailmaker's Darn. This has no relationship to the domestic darn, being the herringbone stitch, as can be seen from the drawing. The secret is to pull the stitching steady, but not too tight.

the illustration in *figure 73* needs no further explanation. Each stitch should not be pulled tighter than is necessary to hold the two sides of the tear together.

Roping. You will usually only need to re-sew a short length of rope on to a mainsail, probably at the headboard or clew. The edge of the sail should be placed over the knees, with the rope to be sewn going across from left to right. Turn up the edge of the cloth through 90° for convenience of sewing, and use the basic round stitch, as shown in *figure 74*. Pass the needle between the lay of the rope, trying not to

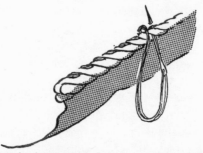

Fig. 74. Roping. Practice is essential before you can become at all good at roping. Even half an hour with a spare bit of rope and canvas will make a world of difference, but don't expect to become expert in under four or five years.

sew through a strand, up through the sail, and back over the top towards you, then back to the first position ready for the next stitch; this passes between the next two strands of rope and the process is repeated. Ten minutes' practice before tackling a sail will repay the effort, and it would be as well to leave anything more than a dozen stitches or so to your sailmaker until you have got more experience. Don't forget to file off the point of your needle to avoid pricking into individual strands of rope at each pass. If the rope has been machined on to the sail, or into a luff tape, you would be advised to try and pick up the old stitch holes (which run straight through the rope) as this will make it both easier and a better job.

Repair Tape. I include repair tape in the section on benchwork because it is another way of holding two parts of cloth together and,

112

therefore, technically counts as stitching. Originally brought in for emergency repairs to spinnakers during racing, it has proved so good that owners tend to leave it for long periods on tears in working sails as well, only getting the job properly done by a sailmaker at the end of the season. This gets you more sailing time and there is nothing against it, providing it does the job properly—which it usually does.

Repairs

I cannot hope to cover here the whole field of possible repairs and must once again refer you to my other book if you want fuller information. Repairs should be done as they occur and certainly before the sails are put away for storage, or you will find that you are well down the sailmaker's queue in the spring. Off-season repairs not only earn you the goodwill of your sailmaker but you will probably get a more careful job as he has more time to spend on them. If you are going to do them yourself, you may require a good deal of the winter to fit them into convenient moments and, indeed, to learn how to cope with some of them. Some of the more common repairs thrown up by the laying-up examination suggested in the previous chapter are listed below.

Don't forget to use a bench hook where you can, in order to steady the work; it will make life easier and the finished job better.

Chafe. Short lengths of machine stitching which need renewing can be re-sewn by hand, often picking up the same needle holes; start well into the good stitching to ensure an ample overlap. Longer lengths should either be oversewn on the machine or, in the case of a seam which has gone, a third row of new machine stitching may be run down between the faulty two. If the actual sailcloth has started to chafe away, either put a small patch over the affected part or, if this is going to be too thick or too heavy (such as at a leech, which needs to be light, or where the headboard rope enters the mast groove and cannot be too thick or it will not pass through the groove), darn the chafe using a standard domestic darn as you would on a pair of socks. Try not to make too many holes as you darn, or you will only weaken the material further; you may find that the darn should only

113

be run in one direction and that the cross stitches should be left out. This repair is often a nice exercise in judgement to assess the amount of stitching to put in as against the possible further weakening effect through making too many holes in a cloth which is already thin. At all events, the final darn should be hammered flat and possibly rubbed with a beeswax block if it is to run in a groove.

Ropes. The most likely rope repairs you will encounter will be to re-sew an end where it has started to come away at headboard or clew. Remove any hide casing by cutting the stitching and place it in water to soak. Half an hour of this while the rope is being re-sewn will soften it to the point where it may be easily worked. Use the ordinary roping stitch already described, and start well into the firm rope so that you have a good anchor. Short lengths of luff tape may be re-sewn by hand, but longer lengths should be put through the machine (this may mean taking off the rope first).

Patches. The best way to repair a tear in a racing sail is to let your sailmaker do it, or you will risk creases. If you are going to patch an old sail yourself, cobble the tear together either by large tacking

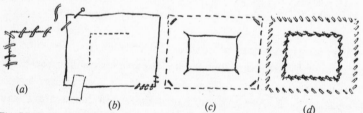

Fig. 75. *Patch.* If you fix the new cloth firmly over the tear before sewing, with warp and weft lined up correctly, there is no reason why a patch should cause creasing of the sail. See that it is very slightly slack rather than tight when it is sewn on.

stitches or with repair tape, draw a rectangle round the area to be patched, and then cut out a piece of cloth about half an inch bigger all round (with the weave running in the same direction) and heat-seal its edges. Place it on the side opposite to the repair tape and pencil outline, and pin it to the sail. Sew round the outside edge of the patch

114

with a sewing machine or by using the hand tabling stitch described above. Now turn the sail over and cut out the affected part along the pencil line using a pair of scissors. Either heat-seal the raw edge with a soldering iron, being careful not to push the end through the new cloth just put on, or else turn the edge under itself and then sew all round again to hold it down. The sequence is shown in *figure 75.*

Worked Eye. A hand-worked eye has two or three times the strength of one which is stamped in with a punch. Place the brass ring at the desired spot and mark its inner and outer circumferences on the sail

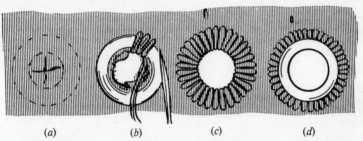

(a)   (b)   (c)   (d)

Fig. 76. Worked Eye. A hand-worked eye is often needed by the dinghy sailer: a Cunningham hole, a cover lashing point, or a new clew ring. Note how the cloth is not cut right away in the middle of the ring, so that something is left for the thread to grip. Punching in the brass turnover to protect the stitching needs special equipment.

with a pencil. Cut away part of the inner circle, leaving some cloth to be sewn into the ring for added strength; a cross cut in the right place will do this best. Lay the ring between the two circumferences again and pass the needle down through the canvas outside the ring at any point on the outer circle. The thread is pulled downwards, leaving a tail to be knotted or sewn over by the first four or five stitches as a stopper, and the needle then brought up through the cut-out and centre of the ring. It is then passed over the top of the ring and down through the pencil line again, moving slightly round the circle each time. A large marlin spike should ideally be pushed into the ring at intervals to keep the canvas spread and the stitches even. Modern practice is to use two parts of thread (four parts on large eyes for bigger boats), spacing the stitches rather wider apart than

115

used to be customary, in order to reduce the danger of wrinkles. When the circle is complete, the last stitch is pushed up and down a couple of times away from the ring, and cut off. A protecting piece called a brassy or turnover is finally punched into the sewn ring to save the stitching from the effects of chafe from shackles, etc. (*figure 76*).

Darning. Darning should be restricted to very small holes no bigger than the end of a cigarette, and should never be used where the canvas is known to be weak. Use a double or even quadruple seaming thread and pass the needle under and over the first layer of stitching you put in, in the usual domestic manner. Note that this is different from the sailmaker's darn described above, which holds two parts of a tear together.

Sailmaker's Whipping. A sailmaker's whipping lasts much longer than an ordinary whipping. Thread a fine needle (number 18) with

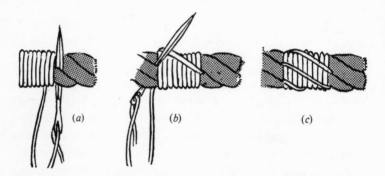

(*a*)   (*b*)   (*c*)

Fig. 77. Sailmaker's Whipping. The secret of a sailmaker's whipping lies in taking the thread across the otherwise completed whipping, and passing it through the lay of the rope and back again. The result will not pull off the end of the rope, and will last indefinitely.

seaming thread, knot the two ends together to form a stopper and so that you put on two parts at once, and wax it if not ready-waxed. Sew once through the lay of the rope as an anchor and then whip in the usual way. Sew between the strands of the rope and out the other side, and then lead the thread back over the whipping along the lay of

116

the rope; sew again between the lay at the other end of the whipping. Lead the thread once again back over the whipping, again along the lay, and back through the strands. Repeat once more until three passes have been made. Sew through the rope to finish off securely. *Figure 77* shows the principle of this whipping.

9 Faults and Alterations

Examining for Faults

When examining a sail for faults, there are some basic rules to follow if you want the most accurate results:

1. A sail will often only show its faults when set on the boat with its matching mainsail or jib and using its normal spars. Examine it afloat first, therefore, and then look at it ashore, either in the dinghy park or on a static test rig. Many sailmakers have a horizontal rig inside the loft, and it can sometimes be most useful to walk all round a sail set in this manner. You can examine at close quarters those parts of the sail which are suspected of giving trouble; you can try the effect of pinching or pulling the cloth in various places and you can usually bend the test mast at will.

2. When sailing, always sight up the mast to see that it is behaving normally *on both tacks* before checking the sail.

3. See that all leech lines are slack or you will get a wrong impression of the sail.

4. Look at the sail from off your boat if possible; at any rate get to leeward and in front of it, for it will often show its faults better from this angle.

5. Write down the faults you find, even marking the positions of creases in pencil on the sail; you will be surprised how inaccurate your memory can be when the sailmaker wants exact details later.

As class competition becomes hotter, special needs require special attention, and minor alterations to new sails are often necessary to get a perfect fit. Give them a chance to settle down first, then let your sailmaker 'breathe' on them to add that touch of greatness which

118

marks the champion. Also, and this is important, do not maltreat your sails and then return them to the loft blaming the sailmaker for faults of your own creation.

A full list of possible faults and the cures for them takes up much more room than we have in this small book. I shall content myself with listing the chief faults and only giving those cures which it is in your power to effect yourself. You will then be able to take action in many cases, and also to observe intelligently those problems which are beyond a do-it-yourself approach.

Mainsail Faults
The chief faults which affect dinghy mainsails are:

Leeches: slack (motorboating or falling away) or tight.
Creases: wrinkles and hard spots other than in the leech.
Fullness: too flat or too full; fullness in the wrong place; back-winding.
Size: too small or too large.

Slack Mainsail Leech. A slack leech is caused by cloth which has stretched locally too much at the leech of the sail. This can be caused by such simple acts as pulling the sail down by the leech instead of by the luff, by treading awkwardly on the sail, or by factors outside your control, such as the sailmaker laying the cloths too much on the bias. Controlled use of a leech line or drawstring can steady a motorboating leech, but avoid overdoing it or you will hook it to windward. The trouble is best cured in the sail loft, and the job of the leech line is to restore the morale of the helmsman by quietening the drumming noise, which can be so distracting. A lot depends on how far in from the leech the sail has stretched. Thus, if the whole leech falls away from the inner ends of the battens, it may either be because the leech cloths have been set by the sailmaker too much on the bias, the sail has too big a roach, or possibly because the sail is not hoisted up hard enough: if there is not enough tension on the luff, there won't be enough on the leech. Before sending the sail back to its maker, try hoisting it a bit harder. If the sail is already out to its marks, a pull down on the Cunningham hole will soon tell you if a tighter luff will

119

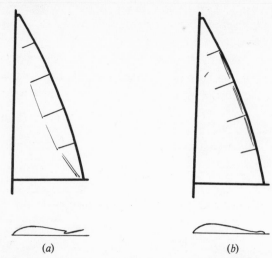

(a)   (b)

Fig. 78. Slack Mainsail Leech. A leech which is slack right into the sail for a good way, will reveal itself by a crease running along the ends of the battens as jn (*a*). The inner ends of the battens tend to poke up to windward, and the sail falls away to leeward from there out to the leech.

If the last 3 or 4 in only are slack, as in (*b*), it is possible that the leech may vibrate in the wind, causing the characteristic drumming noise known as motorboating. The sail may be quite all right apart from this, but there is a danger to morale so get the trouble seen to by your sailmaker.

cure the problem; if it does, you must get your sailmaker to shorten the luff, so you can get more tension on it within the black band distances (*figure 78*).

Tight Mainsail Leech. This is most probably caused in the sail loft by laying the cloths with too little bias at the leech, or by building too much flow too far aft in the sail. It can, however, also be caused by maltreatment by the owner: if you use the sail continuously in hard weather, the flow will be blown aft. In any event, it is a matter for the sailmaker, but before you send the sail back, just make sure that you have not been looking at it all the time with the leech line tight ...

Mainsail Creases. Wrinkles, pleats, and hard spots can come from headboard, eyelets, seams unevenly sewn, a mast which bends too much for a fairly flat sail (*figure 79*), or a dozen other reasons. Many

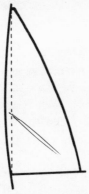

Fig. 79. Flat Sail on a Bendy Mast. If a bendy mast is used with a sail which hasn't got enough cloth built into the luff to allow full movement, mast bend will be restricted. In any case, the mast will remove all flow from the sail as it tries to bend fully, and a crease will run from the clew to the point on the luff where the shortage of cloth is most acute. The cure is to use a stiffer mast, and give your sailmaker accurate offsets next time he makes a mainsail for your bendy mast.

of these faults can be laid at the door of the sailmaker, but synthetic cloth takes a little time to settle down, so always use a new sail for a few hours before complaining; you may find that variation of halyard and outhaul tension will work wonders. Also, before you go rushing off to your sailmaker triumphantly quoting these pages as authority for heaping blame on him willy-nilly, be advised that there are more creases caused by owners than by sailmakers, through maltreatment, wrong setting of the sail, wrong rigging of the spars, wrong information on mast bend before the sails were made, and so on. Finally, creases in synthetics are sometimes almost impossible to avoid, particularly at the clew.

Mainsail Fullness. A sail may have the wrong fullness because, when ordering, you did not compare the fullness you required with that of another suit by the same sailmaker; his idea of flat may be what you mean by medium. Fullness too far forward or aft can be for the same reason. It is easy for a sailmaker to pleat out fullness forward (and the stitching can always be released again if it doesn't do the trick, with no more damage than a few small holes up the luff), and harsh use of a Cunningham hole may draw forward again some of the

121

fullness which has shifted aft. On the other hand, too flat a sail is hard to cure and may be expensive.

Mainsail Backwinding. A mainsail which lifts along the luff whenever you are sailing close hauled is said to be backwinded. This is very often not because the sail is too full forward but because the jib has a curling or bellied leech which is directing wind into the lee side of the mainsail (*figures 8, 9*, and *10*), so don't rush off and have the mainsail flattened before you have looked at the jib leech pretty hard.

Mainsail Size. When a mainsail is spread on the floor without being pulled out along the luff and foot, it will almost certainly measure under size. This is because the cloth is gathered on the rope or tape, which has to be pulled *with tension adequate to remove all wrinkles adjacent to the measurement being taken* (to quote from the I.Y.R.U. Sail Measurement Instructions) before a true picture can be obtained. When failure to pull a sail properly is coupled with the wide variety of methods of getting particular measurements (and take my word for it, some class rules lay down some pretty silly ways of taking certain measurements), you can see how mistakes can occur. Don't, therefore, jump to conclusions when deciding sail size, but call in an expert.

Jib Faults
A jib suffers from much the same faults as a mainsail, and I shall save space if I don't run through them all again. It is worth mentioning the question of size, however, because of a slightly different problem brought on by the luff wire. Here again the sail has to be pulled to its full length on the luff before the measurement is taken. Reference to *figure 80* will show how the sail can appear fully stretched, but only by feel can you tell that the luff wire is snaking inside the luff tabling and is not taut, and therefore the canvas on the luff is not pulled to full length. The mistake is more obvious with control luff jibs, but take care to remove all wrinkles when stretching the luff for measurement.

Spinnaker Faults
Spinnakers are usually made of nylon, and the elastic nature of the thin canvas (don't forget that all sailcloth is canvas: flax, cotton,

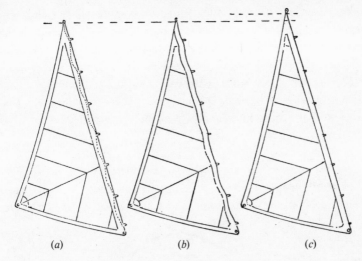

Fig. 80. Jib Luff Measurement. In jib (*a*) the luff is not pulled enough to stretch the cloth, and the luff wire is loose inside the tabling (except where it is seized by the hanks). The sail appears short, but the dotted line shows the wire. Jib (*b*) is similar, but the luff is seized to the luff wire along its length, so easily shows the kinks. Jib (*c*) shows both the previous sails pulled hard out to straighten the wire and get full length, thus also inducing flow in the luff.

duck, polyester, or nylon) means that it can absorb a good many wrinkles in everything but the lightest winds.

Nearly all spinnakers suffer from being too narrow in the head. What looks like a narrow-gutted, spiky affair when viewed from behind in your own boat, however, appears to your rival as a high-breasted beauty bursting with power when seen from in front as, indeed, his sail looks to you. The cure for this universal problem is to get off your own boat once in a while and look at your spinnaker through somebody else's eyes just to revive your morale. If you really do have a narrow-gutted sail, console yourself with the thought that it should set well on a reach and have a low knock-down effect due to its smaller area aloft.

Apart from this overriding defect, spinnaker faults can be fairly evenly divided into three categories.

Head Girts. These stem from an attempt to cram too much cloth into the sail in order to get the biggest area within the rule. After allowing

123

a decent interval for the sail to settle down and solve its own problems, the cure lies in cutting away some of the surplus cloth in the head: this is a matter for the expert. It is interesting that ultra-light weather spinnakers are often made fairly narrow in the head, especially for bigger boats, when you might think that every square inch of area would be vital. Spinnakers with more area, however, also have more weight to lift in ghosting conditions, and they do not fill as quickly as smaller sails.

Tight Stays. Stay is another word for the luff/leech of a spinnaker; if they are tight they curl and offer a poor aerodynamic shape when reaching (*figure 81*). The trouble is usually caused by the cloth just

Fig. 81. Curling Spinnaker Stays. If the tapes on the edges of a spinnaker become shorter than the length of cloth, the stays (luff and leech) will curl inwards to give a poor aerodynamic shape. You can also recognise this fault by a lot of tiny wrinkles running out from the tapes for an inch or so into the sail, where the nylon is gathered along the stays.

inside the edge of the sail stretching, while the tape or wire running the length of the stay remains constant. Cure is a matter for the sailmaker.

Porosity. Spinnaker nylon is very thin and has to be of high quality if it is to stop air passing through it too quickly. Chemical fillers (resins) often dress an otherwise indifferent cloth to a passable stage in its early life, but these will eventually break down (according to care, quality, and amount of use) and the sail will lose a good deal of drive through too much porosity. The cure lies in selecting a good cloth when you buy a sail.

Alterations

Alterations which can be made to sails cover such a wide range that I shall reluctantly have to skim the surface and only touch on those

124

aspects which have most bearing on the alteration of second-hand sails to fit another boat. A 5–0–5 or Fireball mainsail is made to the same stretched sizes the world over and, since I assume that an owner would not go outside his class for second-hand sails, alterations to one-design sails do not really apply (unless they were made to the wrong sizes, when minor surgery will usually bring them into line). Interest in this part of the book, therefore, will be limited to those classes like the 14-ft International or the Flying Dutchman which can vary the size of sails within their rule, and also to owners of knockabout dinghies who are keen to add cheaply to their wardrobe.

Mainsails. If a mainsail needs enlarging, a great deal depends not only on how much bigger it has to be made but also which cut has been used to make it: horizontal, mitre, radial, or vertical. Generally speaking, enlargements are neither easy nor cheap, and any saving which you may enjoy through buying second-hand will be more than swallowed up by the alterations. Reductions, however, can more easily be done, but care has to be taken when re-cutting the leech not to leave the unsupported cloth too much on the bias or it will stretch.

Mainsail Foot. The foot can sometimes be shortened by cutting in at the clew and fairing to the first or second batten pocket, depending

Fig. 82. Shortening the Mainsail Foot. It is a fairly simple matter to chop an inch or so off the length of the foot at the clew. How high up the leech the sail will have to be faired off will depend on how much is taken off and also on the amount of roach on the leech.

125

on how much is taken off (*figure 82*). The least that can be taken off is about an inch, to a point just inside the clew eye, because anything less would cut through the middle of the eye and leave a gap at the leech.

Mainsail Half Height. The half height can easily be reduced by half an inch or so through pleating the luff (which will draw in the leech), but remember that this will also flatten the sail; if more is required, it will have to be cut off the leech, which will then have to be faired above and below the half height, possibly for most of the length of the leech (*figure 83*). The foot will probably also have to be shortened if

Fig. 83. *Reducing the Mainsail Half-height Width*. If the sail is trimmed off at the leech to reduce the cross measurement, the amount of reduction will determine how far up and down the sail the leech will have to be faired. In any event, at least two batten pockets will have to be lifted and put back again.

the half height is too much, so you can count on the whole leech being altered; this means taking off and replacing all batten pockets, besides remaking the leech itself.

Mainsail Luff. Reducing the luff usually means taking off the top foot or so of rope and the headboard, cutting off the appropriate amount of luff, and replacing the headboard and rope. The leech also has to be attended to, as a glance at *figure 84 (a)* will show. The job can also be done by cutting up at the tack as in *figure 84 (b)*, but this means that the boom will droop more, because the leech is undisturbed and remains its original length despite the shorter luff. In addition, the whole rope has to come off for this method, so it is much more expensive. A quicker way altogether, where only an inch or so is involved, is to oversew the bolt rope by hand for its entire length; the action of pulling the stitches tight will cause the rope to shorten and take the sail with it.

                 (a)   (b)

Fig. 84. Shortening the Mainsail Luff. A mainsail luff may be shortened by cutting a piece off at the head (*a*) or tack (*b*). If the head is cut, the leech will also be shortened and the clew will be lifted the same amount as the luff is shortened—usually a good thing. If the tack is cut, the leech stays the same, and the boom will then droop. If system (*a*) is used to shorten the luff by a lot, care must be taken that the cloths won't then meet the re-cut upper leech at too great an angle; if they do, this part of the sail slackens and it would be better to find another way to make the alteration.

Bendy/Stiff Mast. A sail which was made for a bendy mast can have some of the convex round trimmed or pleated out of the luff, to adapt it for a stiffer spar. To alter the sail the other way means adding cloth to the luff, and is not possible without major expense and risk of failure.

Jibs. The most important part of the jib is the leech. If this is flat and without a curl at the tabling, you are 90 per cent of the way towards a good sail. Any alteration to such a jib, therefore, should leave this vital part undisturbed if possible. You can see from *figures 85* and *86*

127

Fig. 85. Shortening a Jib Foot. It is not as hard a job as it may seem, to take the luff wire out of a jib, cut the sail as shown in this drawing and then replace the wire; this shortens the foot and leaves the leech undisturbed. The alternative is to cut the sail at the clew, which runs the risk of spoiling the leech, as it has to be faired almost all the way to the head.

Fig. 86. Shortening a Jib on both Luff and Leech. If the luff is cut in at the head, rather than the tack, the leech will be shortened at the same time as the luff. The resulting sail will have a higher clew, because the angle of the luff will be altered.

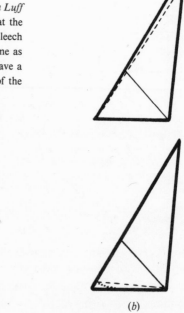

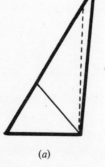

(a)

(b)

Fig. 87. Shortening a Jib Luff. If it is important to leave the clew at the same place when shortening a jib luff, the sail must be cut as in (a), with all the dangers attached to altering a leech. Cutting up at the tack as in (b) will lower the clew, but present small danger to the set of the sail. This latter alteration can often be done with little loss of area if the opportunity is taken to put a lot of round, or roach, on the foot (dotted line).

128

how the foot can be shortened and how the luff and leech can be shortened together, both safe alterations as far as not disturbing the leech is concerned; both are fairly cheap, but note that both leave the jib at a different angle on the forestay, so your sheet lead position will have to change. If you want to shorten the luff, you may cut in at the head or tack as shown in *figures 87 (a)* and (*b*); the first method disturbs the leech (which can be all right if it is not excessive, but is always a risk) and the second lowers the clew nearer to the deck. Almost all other alterations to a jib are either costly or dangerous, or both.

Spinnakers. The most common alteration to a dinghy spinnaker is to cut down a fairly old sail for use in heavy weather. The sail can be

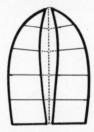

Fig. 88. Making a Spinnaker Narrower and Flatter. If the centre seam of a spinnaker is undone, the sail will then be in two halves, and making it narrower is simply a question of trimming the right amount from the middle and joining the two halves again to remake the centre seam. Taking rather more cloth from the upper half will flatten the head.

split down the middle and made narrower and flatter, particularly in the head, as in *figure 88*; it can also be taken apart at the first cloth above the foot for something to be taken off the length of the stays (*figure 89*). Both these alterations leave the stays undisturbed except for length and don't mean making new clews. They are, therefore, fairly safe and cheap. Even a spherical spinnaker (one with no vertical centre seam) can be safely split down the middle in this way, provided you don't mind having a vertical centre seam when the job is done; the alternative is the more costly one of taking half the reduction off each side and fitting new luff/leech tapes and new clews.

129

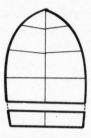

Fig. 89. Shortening a Spinnaker on the Stays. Similarly, if the first horizontal seam above the foot is undone, a parallel piece can be taken out to shorten the height of the sail. This means that the two clews are left undisturbed and don't have to be undone and remade, so it is a fairly economical alteration.

Second-hand Sails

Talk of alteration leads naturally to thoughts about second-hand sails. As I said above, you should be careful when buying sails which were not made for your sizes, because you may wind up paying enough for the alterations to have enabled you to buy new sails in the first place.

The first question to ask when buying second-hand sails is why they are being sold. If there is no convincing reason, the suspicion must be that they do not set very well; perhaps they look all right to the untutored eye, but the flow may have been blown aft to an inefficient place through persistent use in strong winds.

Next, examine the sail as though for laying up as suggested on pages 105–6. Then look for pleats and empty stitch holes. A pleat will show that the sail has been flattened, while empty stitch holes, particularly at the leech, betray alterations which may mean that the set of the sail is suspect.

The sail should now be set on your own boat and taken afloat for a trial. If it fits, examine it for creases and fullness as listed at the beginning of this chapter—and make sure that you have a look at it in both light and strong winds. If it doesn't fit, don't take the word of the seller (or the evidence of this book) that the alteration will be easy and cheap, but take the sail to a sailmaker and ask him for a quotation for the job.

130

New Sails

If, after reading this book, you decide that nothing less than a new suit of sails will please you, yet you have never ordered such a thing before, how do you go about it?

First, select your sailmaker. Questions of price and quality, specialisation and location will all play their part in this. Ask around the clubhouse, have a look at other people's sails, and consult your bank account. Remember that a loft near at hand can help a lot if you think you will want after-sales service. If you already have a sailmaker, it should take a lot to make you decide to leave him; the devil you know ...

When you have made your choice, be content to put yourself in his hands. He has dealt with all sorts of customers before, and it is unlikely that you can surprise him. Besides basic information on fullness required and any cloth preferences you have, accurate details of your spars are vital for a good fit, and information on crew weight will reveal how much power you can expect to control. If your class of boat is not well known, it is worth asking if he has all the latest amendments to the rules (some class secretaries are bad at circulating sailmakers with rule alterations affecting sails). Ask for a sample of the cloth the sailmaker proposes using, and tell him of any extras you want: window, racing number, boat's name on the sailbag, special set of battens for light weather, and so on.

Like tailors, sailmakers do not always have the best reputation for prompt delivery, but if you order in plenty of time and allow a small margin on the promise you get, you should not often be disappointed—especially if you drop him a reminder just before the sails are due. Ordering in the off season not only ensures that you have your new sails by the spring but also often gets you the benefit of seasonal discounts.

While new synthetic sails do not need breaking in as cotton ones did, they will be the better for careful use during the first three or four hours of their life. You may hoist and race with them straight away, but try at least to get half an hour cruising up and down on a reach before the gun goes. I always advise against reefing new sails in their first four hours of sailing. Despite all these warnings, you can misuse synthetics for limited periods and they won't let you down, but if you consistently neglect them you will pay for it in the long run.

Once again, sails are the power unit of a sailing boat, which wouldn't get far without them. Look after them and they will repay your attention.